MOUNT ATHOS

A Journey of Self-Discovery

Luiz Rocha

iUniverse, Inc.
New York   Bloomington

Mount Athos, A Journey of Self-Discovery

iUniverse books may be ordered through booksellers or by contacting:

iUniverse
1663 Liberty Drive
Bloomington, IN 47403
www.iuniverse.com
1-800-Authors (1-800-288-4677)

ISBN: 978-1-4401-1753-4 (pbk)
ISBN: 978-1-4401-1754-1 (ebk)

Printed in the United States of America

iUniverse rev. date: 02/20/2009

TIMELINE

BC	
490	Battle of Marathon. The Athenians defeat the Persian invasion.
480	King Xerxes builds Xerxes's canal and invades Greece again. Decisive Greek victory ends Persian presence in Europe.
45	Julius Caesar introduces the calendar which took his name.
AD	
64	Persecution of Christians by Nero at Rome.
312	Battle of the Milvian Bridge in Rome. Constantine adopts Christianity.
313	Constantine issues the Edict of Milan, accepting the Christian religion.
325	First Ecumenical Council of Nicaea.
330	Dedication of Constantinople as the Christian new Rome. Birth of the Byzantine (Eastern Roman) Empire.
380	Second Ecumenical Council of Constantinople.
431	Third Ecumenical Council at Ephesus.
451	Fourth Ecumenical Council at Chalcedon.
537	Dedication of Hagia Sophia in Constantinople.
553	Fifth Ecumenical Council at Constantinople.
681	Sixth Ecumenical Council at Constantinople.
726	Outbreak of iconoclastic controversy.
787	Seventh Ecumenical Council in Nicaea.
843	Restoration of the use of icons by Byzantine empress Theodora.
885	The Byzantine emperor recognizes Athos as a territory belonging to the monks.

TIMELINE

AD	
1054	The Great Schism between the Orthodox and Catholic Churches.
1060	Byzantine edict establishes basic conditions for admission into Athos.
1095-1099	First Crusade.
1146-1148	Second Crusade.
1188-1192	Third Crusade fails to recapture Jerusalem.
1198-1204	Fourth Crusade. Crusaders capture and sack Constantinople.
1261	Michael VIII enters Constantinople and restores the Byzantine Empire.
1430-1460	Flowering of Byzantine arts and Platonism; migration of Byzantine scholars and artists to Western Europe.
1453	Siege and capture of Constantinople by Mehmet II. The end of the Byzantine Empire.
1582	The Gregorian calendar is decreed by Pope Gregory XIII.
1616	Galileo Galilei is condemned by the Roman Catholic Holy Inquisition.
1923	Treaty of Lausagne recognizes Athos's autonomy with Greek sovereignty.
1964	Orthodox and Catholic Churches lift a 1,000-year-old excommunication.

Contents

1

PAGAN PATHWAYS

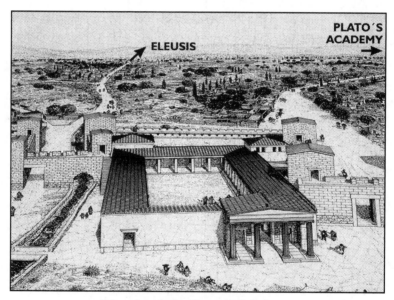

The Ancient Gates of Athens

I stood in Athens in front of the ancient city walls and its two main gates. One was leading to Plato's Academy, the other to Eleusis.

The Academy is one of the two supreme achievements of Plato, the other being the immortalizing of Socrates in writing. Both have profoundly influenced the Western world. Plato had a clear vision of what he wanted to achieve with the Academy: to educate young men and women to seek the truth, with the hope that they would be qualified to assume positions of leadership in the world where they could put that truth to work. He was convinced that men will stop fighting only when they understand the truth about things. He said, "Until philosophers are kings or kings have the spirit and power of philosophy, the human race will never rest from their evils."

At that time as I faced the gates of Athens, my objectives were less philosophical and more spiritual. My whole day had been dedicated to visiting Eleusis and to traveling along the 20km of the Sacred Way, the ancient road from Eleusis to Athens. Eleusis was the place where the Mysteries of Eleusis were celebrated for 1,500 years until they were abolished by the Byzantine emperor in 391 AD. The central theme of the mysteries was man's eternal yearning for immortality and it was related to the symbolic death of vegetation in the Earth's uterus during winter and its triumphal rebirth in spring. The ancients saw in the yearly birth-maturity-death-resurrection cycle of the vegetation their own life cycle.

The mysteries were charged with emotional intensity. The rituals attracted thousands of initiates every spring. At the end of the rite the temple was in complete darkness. At the climatic moment the priestess would appear with the sacred fire brought from the mystery room under the temple and would pass it on to the initiates, from one to another, illuminating their unlit torches. The temple became ablaze and at that moment the neophytes had a personal direct contact with the divine. They would leave in procession to Athens, headed by the priestess and the sacred symbols of worship, along the Sacred Way, all shouting, "Iero, iero, iero" (holy, holy, holy). Their feelings and beliefs were summarized by Sophocles, who said, "Fortunate are those mortals who, after having contemplated and experienced the Mysteries, are going down to the other life. There, only they will be in ecstasy. The others, only agony will have."

As thousands of faithful had done for centuries, I left Eleusis for Athens along the Sacred Way. On the top of the hill between Eleusis and Athens I visited a church where once existed a temple dedicated to Apollo. The church was built using the pagan temple's materials. This sort of appropriation became very common after the legalization of Christianity and Christians. In order to express their beliefs, they employed the figurative language of the age, borrowing familiar forms from the Greco-Roman world and imbuing new significance for further propagation of the faith.

Seventeen centuries after the mysteries have been abolished, every spring the Orthodox Church celebrates Easter. The churches are packed for the Saturday Resurrection service. Ten minutes before midnight the lights are put out. The temple is in complete darkness. Suddenly the priest appears at the central door of the sanctuary with the "holy fire." The Orthodox ritual of the "holy fire" dates back at least 1,200 years. It is performed alone by a patriarch in the tomb of Jesus in Jerusalem. The fire is then taken aboard a special flight to Athens and distributed to all churches in Greece.

From this flame brought by the priest the candles of the congregation are lit and passed from one to another until the church is ablaze. As the congregation leaves, a river of light pours out of the temple's doors, one faithful saying "Christos Anesti" (Christ is risen) and the other replying "Alithos Anesti" (He has really risen). As in the past they have experienced a mystery and they go home carrying their candles illuminated and with the certainty of their resurrection as brought in Christ's message.

The similarities between the Mysteries of Eleusis and the final Orthodox Easter liturgy are so astonishing that we can say that the religiosity of the initiated in the mysteries is not at all unlike that of their present Christian Orthodox descendants. Interestingly most of what we know about the Mysteries of Eleusis came from Christian authors who were trying to defend their faith from such assessments.

The Orthodox Church still maintains the rituals of early Christianity, which were highly influenced by paganism. Participating in the Orthodox liturgies is like rewinding 1,700 years on the wheels of time. And this spiritual link between past and present was one of the reasons I chose Greece for my pilgrimage.

In front of those gates and the quietude surrounding them, my mind traveled to a few months before when I was completely stressed. I felt that my speed was so high I did not have the time to appreciate the scenery around me and I was missing the whole meaning of life. It happens to all of us—suddenly we sense that we've been playacting in a drama written by a hand other than our own and the script no longer works. What this moment requires is a journey, to leave the surface of our lives and descend into our interior. Fortunately I listened to the voice from within calling for something different, for a short-term rupture with my present and my past as a way of realigning myself. That was the reason for my pilgrimage.

When I finally crossed the portals of ancient Athens, I heard the bells of the nearby Orthodox church. I felt like I was traversing some mystic entryway to my real destination, an enclave in Greece that has been dedicated to monastic life since the times of the Byzantine Empire. It is a place molded in tradition, history, legend, and miracles. Known as Mount Athos, it remains fundamentally unchanged since the eighth century.

2

THE CITY OF HEAVENS
OURANOPOLIS

The long and winding road from Athens had come to an end at Ouranopolis, a small village by the sea with some houses, shops, and taverns huddling around a Byzantine tower. A gentle breeze was coming from the sea, the sun preparing to settle down, and the sound of crickets attracted me with their consonant and dissonant notes.

There is no other place on Earth but in Greece where the crickets sing with such a vibration and strength, creating hypnotic and relaxing sounds so characteristic of the summer in Greece. It seems like they are in an eternal quest for a summer symphony. They start in a solo mode, each one trying to find its tune. Some sing softly, some fast. Some sing with deep notes, some with acute notes. And all of a sudden they come together consonantly for a while and then there is a pause, as a needed relaxation, to start all over again later on. The crickets are like us, each of them trying to find and tune its role in this vast universe. In Ouranopolis though they seemed to have a special meaning. The crickets were there performing their concert and, like a welcoming committee to Athos, they were saying, "Fellows, it's time to find the tune of your lives."

I was sitting at a tavern by the sea, sipping an ouzo, having some appetizers, and thinking about the long route I had traveled all the way from Rio de Janeiro to Ouranopolis. I knew that if you are following either your inner call, your dream, or your goal, the more distant the destination, the more empowered you feel when you are getting closer to it. And from my chair I could see Mount Athos far away on the horizon.

"It's beautiful, isn't it?" said the old lady who was serving me, pointing to the mountain that could be seen further south. "That's the Garden of the Virgin Mary, the most sacred place in Greece. After she touched that soil, no more women were allowed there."

Saying that, she immediately made the sign of the cross three times and continued, "Greece is a country blessed by God and our religion, Orthodoxy, a religion preserving most of the credo and rituals from early Christianity. And do you know the meaning of our village's name?" she asked. Without waiting for an answer, she replied, "Ouranopolis means 'the city of heavens,' very appropriate since we are so close to this sacrosanct place. Before my husband died, he used to go there many times during the year with my son. Now my son is going there with my two grandsons. People who are going there for the first time, they all have this look, like yours, of 'What am I going to find there?' Don't worry, you will like it . . . . It is your first time, isn't it?" she asked.

Before I took a breath to answer, she had gone to the kitchen. Observing the sun falling into the Aegean Sea, I came back to my thoughts, emotions, and feelings. I felt inspired, curious, and anxious to respond to this inner call from my pilgrim soul that had begun probably 20 years ago when I saw an article about the Greek consul in Rio de Janeiro, Brazil, describing his yearly pilgrimages to Athos. He mentioned that Mount Athos is one of the oldest surviving monastic communities in the world, an exclusive domain of monks and other holy men, the spiritual center of the Orthodox Church.

The years passed by and I noticed that every Greek Orthodox man whom I met had at least once during his life visited Athos. It seemed like an initiation ceremony associated with their Greek roots. By then I thought that Athos was more of a Greek realm for Greeks until two years ago when I read that Prince Charles, heir to the British throne, visits this monastic community every year and that he had started a project to maintain an ancient network of mule tracks and footpaths between the monasteries. I got curious to know why he openly expresses his predilection for Orthodoxy and seeks inner peace in Athos.

This curiosity began my process of trying to understand more about Athos, just to find out that Athos is not only Greek but international. From the 20 ruling monasteries, 17 are Greek, 1 Russian, 1 Bulgarian, and 1 Serbian. Mount Athos is an enclave in Greece, governed by Christian Orthodox monks. In spiritual terms Athos is not of this world at all. For more than a thousand years it has been a part of Europe entirely devoted to monastic life and to nothing else. In 885 AD the Byzantine emperor issued an imperial edict officially recognizing Athos as a territory belonging exclusively to monks. It declared that only religious men should live there. After the fall of the Constantinople in 1453 AD, which brought Mount Athos under the occupation of the Ottoman Empire that lasted for 460 years, the rights of the monasteries in "the country in which day and night the name of God is revered" were recognized in edicts issued by the sultans from the Ottoman Empire. During this period Athos became a center for preservation of the Greek culture and heritage. The monks supported and even fought at the war of independence of Greece, initiated in 1821, and finally Athos was liberated by the Greek army from the Ottomans in 1913. Their autonomy with Greek sovereignty was ratified by the Treaty of Lausagne in 1923.

The basic conditions for admission into Athos are defined in an edict issued by the Byzantine emperor in 1060 AD. It decrees that women are never admitted, a permit is required for anyone entering the territory, and overnight stay is forbidden except for those who have proven religious or scientific interests and are over 18 years old. The procedure to obtain the appropriate permit takes some time. There is a daily quota of 120 Orthodox pilgrims and 10 non-Orthodox. You must apply well in advance.

"Why are you here?" asked the old lady.

"Well, making a long story short, the first time I heard about Athos was 20 years ago. During the following years I understood more and more about Athos and six months ago I decided that I could not delay any more. And here I am ready to visit this sacred place."

"It is not a visit, my son," she said. "This will be a journey deep into your soul and I assure you that you will be touched. I have not seen anyone who has not been inspired by going to Athos. My husband used to say that each time he went to Athos was a unique experience. He was always learning something different from each of the monks he met."

An old man was passing by and the old lady called him. He was her brother. She told him that I was Brazilian and that she was trying to explain to me about Athos. The old man looked carefully at me, at her, sat on a chair at my table, and after a few moments he said, "Do not listen to women. They do not know what they are saying. Let me tell you in a simple sentence what Athos is all about: Believe and you will find it. Did you get it?" he asked. "Believe and you will find it," he repeated. "And now let's talk about Brazilian soccer. Do you know that there are many Brazilian soccer players in Greece?"

And I ended my day surrounded by three more Greeks in a lively conversation about soccer. That was weird. I was in the process of a spiritual renewal, miles away from Rio, and I ended my day discussing mundane topics such as Brazilian soccer. Well, this is part of life indeed; you may have a goal, but the

music by the famous Greek composer Mikis Theodorakis. The all-encompassing theme of the poem is that the essence of man's humanity is his ability to hold opposites, his ability to survive as neither angel nor devil, sensualist nor saint, but as something beyond, assimilating both. And this is the heart of Greek sensibility, its capacity for balancing the world of senses and the world of spirit." He excused himself and went to talk to an old friend.

I waited among the mass of people eager to board the ferry and studied my surroundings with curiosity. "I am in a land where spirituality, poetry, and music fuse together in an unique word like in the ancient Pan-Hellenic games when art and spirituality were always together. If such is the explanation for the ferry's name, imagine what I will get in Athos. . . , " I thought.

After the last of the eager passengers boarded, the ferry *Axion Esti* slowly left the pier to Dafni in Athos, a two-hour trip along the coast. Set on the easternmost promontory of the three Halkidiki peninsulas, which jut like spread fingers into the Aegean Sea, Athos's rugged territory of sheer cliffs and forests consists of a range which runs southeast for 56 km from Xerxes's Canal. Dominating its southern end, the snow-capped summit of Athos itself peaks to 2,000 meters before dropping into the sea.

From the ferry Ouranopolis was getting smaller and smaller. On the deck we were a community of pilgrims gradually leaving the 21st century behind. We were leaving the secular world and entering into a spiritual realm where people have dedicated their entire lives to reflecting about the ultimate question of all mankind and yet it must be reopened by each of us: "What is the meaning of existence?" This question branches into many practical ones such as "What does it mean to be human and fully alive? How can we make life worth living? How can we find inner comfort in the stressful, swirling circumstances of life?" Sometimes whispered, sometimes screamed, we know that these have no easy answers, but the act of reflecting on them make us leave the surface of our lives and descend into our interior in search of the path that will lead us to ourselves once again.

Viktor Frankl in his autobiographical work, *Man's Search for Meaning*, explains that the most important driver in a person's life is the quest for meaning because "everything can be taken from man but one thing, the last of the human freedoms: to choose one's attitude in any given set of circumstances, to choose one's own way no matter the circumstance." Through the ages man has sought clues to life's meaning through religion and philosophy, and Athos is one of these guiding places in helping us decide what shall become of us, mentally and spiritually.

I was sitting on a bench with the same Orthodox priest who had explained the ferry's name to me. He had recently been ordained in the US. At a certain point he said, "Look , that is the Xerxes' canal. By the end of the sixth century BC, the Persians were by far the strongest power in the eastern Mediterranean region, ruling as far as Egypt and India. To their king, Darius, it appeared both inevitable and easy to extend the Persian power west. In 492 BC a Persian fleet was destroyed by a storm as it tried to round the Athos peninsula on its way to invade Greece. In 490 BC the Persians returned and were defeated at Marathon. The Persians, astonished, retired for 10 years, returning under the personal leadership of Darius's successor, Xerxes. In another trial to defeat Greece, King Xerxes left nothing to chance."

He shifted on the bench to avoid facing the bright sun directly. "Xerxes ordered his men to build a canal through the isthmus of Athos rather than risk his fleet on the rocks at its southern point. This immense operation took three years to complete and it was one of the biggest engineering wonders of its time. In 480 BC the canal was opened in the presence of King Xerxes himself and the empire's ships passed through on their way to the conquest of Greece. The Persian fleet was defeated by Sparta and Athens at Salamis and in 479 BC the

Greeks destroyed the Persian military power at Platea, ending the Persian presence in Europe.

"How did the Greeks defeat the greatest army in the world, a force 10 times their number, not just once but many times over a period of years? The Greeks observed that the Persian soldiers and sailors often had to be whipped into battle while the Greek discipline was that of free men, able to choose. They fought because they wished to, not because they were forced to. And they decided never to give in for that would betray their freedom.

"The channel was forgotten and abandoned but remained as a symbol of our Western idea of what it means to be free. The wall you can see along the canal is 2km long and separates Greece from Athos. That is the minimum width of Athos, which broadens to a maximum of 8 along its 56km length."

"Have you been to Athos many times?" I asked.

"Yes. Before my ordination I was coming to Athos once a year."

"And how did you decide to be a priest?"

"This is a vocation that I felt at a certain point in my life. I was already married. I spoke openly with my wife and she supported my decision. In Orthodoxy, for the lower ranks of the priesthood, celibacy is not mandatory and you can have a normal life with a family. Although the Orthodox can marry up to three times, priests can marry only once and that must occur before their ordination."

"And your trip to Athos is something mandatory after ordination?" I persisted.

"No, but Athos is a very sacred place and interacting with the monks can be very inspiring and a way of learning from people who are deeper into their spirituality. But tell me," he continued, "you are not an Orthodox, are you?"

"No, I am a Catholic by birth, but I do believe that all religions are different lenses through which to look at God. The paths can

15

be many although the end is only one. Do you think that being a Catholic will be a problem?" I frowned slightly.

"In early Christianity the Church was only one but now is split among many. The Orthodox and the Roman Catholic Churches have been separated since 1054 because of some theological issues and, why not say, power disputes as well. But I believe that the sacking of Constantinople by the Fourth Crusaders, which lead to the fall of the city into the hands of the Ottoman Empire, was the decisive event to create the rift and the resentment between the two churches for so long. In 1964 the Orthodox and the Catholic Churches lifted a mutual 1,000-year-old excommunication. Despite the fact that they have maintained since then a constructive dialog to find ways of getting unified again, this task will not be easy. But even if they do not succeed, their approximation is a good thing resulting from the process. However you will see in Athos some monasteries more receptive to Catholics than others. And this selection was naturally made when you applied to get your permit, which means that you will not have problems during your stay. What may happen is that in some of the monasteries they may not let you participate in the liturgies."

He paused while I pondered his comments. "And now tell me," he continued, "what are you looking for in Athos?"

"I have always had an admiration for Greece and for all that in the ancient Greek culture which was pivotal in forming our Western civilization. Many years ago I heard about Athos and got curious about this place. At this point I would say that I am more intrigued than anything else and at the same time remember what Socrates said 2,500 years ago that 'an unexamined life is not worth living.' Athos must be the kind of place where introspection and self-evaluation are facilitated."

"For sure it is," he agreed. "But something deeper in your soul brought you here. Maybe you do not know yet what this is, but you will find and be touched by it. Athos is neither a land of curiosity nor mundane things but a sanctified place where you will get closer to your spiritual being. Keep this in your mind and open your heart to this unique experience."

And while we talked, the landscape became unspoiled with wooded peaks interspersed with precipitous ravines, the blue sea bathing the shore and seagulls following our ferry. On the way to Dafni the ferry called at the Bulgarian monastery of Zografou and at the Greek monasteries of Doriachou and Xenofondos. The monasteries were sort of a refuge surrounded by cultivated plots in the middle of the wilderness. On the window of one of those I saw a banner with the saying, "Orthodoxy or death." Two thousand years after the Christian message has been spread around and the Bible has become one of the all-time bestsellers, how easy it is yet for some people to misinterpret it and consider themselves as part of one club against another instead of belonging to a greater and unified flock.

When we called at the Russian monastery of Pandeleimonos, the church clock indicated 14:40hs, three hours ahead of Greek time.

I said to the priest, pointing to the clock, "Look at the tower clock. I believe that the Russians are using Russian time instead of the Greek time!"

"Do not bring your mindset to Athos," he warned. "This is a different world and the daily lives and religious practices of the monks are according to strict Byzantine rules, unaltered throughout the centuries. The day is divided between sunrise and sunset. Sunset is equivalent to midnight while sunrise is noon. Depending on the season, clocks will be between three to six hours ahead of Greek time. The Julian calendar is still being used so that their date is behind the rest of the world. Christmas, for example, is celebrated 14 days late."

Puzzled, I asked, "What is the difference between the calendars?"

"Two main versions of the Christian calendar have existed: the Julian and the Gregorian. The difference between them lies in the way they approximate the length of the tropical year (this is the time taken for Earth's rotation around the sun) and their rules for calculating Easter. The Julian calendar was introduced by Julius Caesar in 45 BC.

"Until that time priest-astronomers were assigned the duty of declaring when a new month began. During those years in Rome a priest observed the sky and announced a new moon and therefore the new month to the king or emperor. According to Suetonius, a prominent Roman historian and biographer, 'The pontiffs had allowed the calendar to fall into such disorder, by intercalating days or months as it suited them, that the harvest and vintage festivals no longer corresponded with the appropriate seasons.' For centuries afterwards Romans referred to the first day of each new month as *Kalends* from their word *calare* (to announce solemnly, to call out). The word *calendar* came from this custom. In Greece today it is still very common on the first day of the month to salute each other with 'Have a good month.'"

He continued explaining that "The Julian calendar was in common use until the 16th century AD. It considered the tropical year approximated as 365.25 days, giving an error of 1 day in approximately 128 years. The Gregorian calendar, commonly used today, was decreed by Pope Gregory XIII to correct for errors in the Julian calendar. In the Gregorian calendar the tropical year is approximated as 365.2425 days, taking approximately 3,300 years for the tropical year to shift 1 day. The papal bull of February 1582 decreed that 10 days should be dropped from October 1582 so that 15 October should follow immediately after 4 October, and from then on the reformed calendar should be used. This was observed in Italy, Poland, Portugal, and Spain at first. Other Catholic countries followed shortly after, but Protestant countries took more time to change and the Orthodox countries didn't change until 1923."

"I touched on one of his favorites topics" I thought, while he continued with his explanation.

"The Orthodox Church does not celebrate Easter on the same day as the Catholics and Protestants because they use the Julian calendar when calculating Easter. In the case of Athos they still use entirely the Julian calendar, which gives dates for Easter that are different even from the Orthodox Church.

"In 1997 representatives of several churches and Christian world communions suggested a common approach to solve the discrepancies between Easter calculations in the Western and the Eastern churches which have been in discussion for centuries, but the solution was once more postponed.

He concluded saying that "Apart from the discussion of Easter, Athos continues to maintain the Julian calendar adopted during the early days of Christianity so that this community is separated from this world in time and space."

I was amazed with the explanation. Some of the things that we take for granted took centuries to be organized. From our perspective we have a feeling like "How is it possible that it took so long for people to get an agreement about this?" Although the process of questioning and answering is part of our humanity, some wrong answers can be maintained for a long time because the right one is considered a menace to the established order by an individual or controlling group that might feel affected by it.

Galileo Galilei (1564-1642), for example, supported the Copernican theory that the Earth was revolving around the sun and not the opposite. In 1610 Galileo Galilei, after observing the planet Jupiter for three days with his telescope, demolished the geocentric worldview. Six years later he was condemned by the Roman Catholic Holy Inquisition office on charges that "the view that the sun stands motionless at the center of the universe is foolish, philosophically false, and utterly heretical because [it is] contrary to the Holy Scripture." In 1992, 350 years after Galileo's death, Pope John Paul II admitted the error on behalf of the Church. As Galileo wrote once, "I do not feel obliged to believe that the same God who has endowed us with sense, reason and intellect has intended us to forgo their use."

We finally arrived at Dafni, a place which is busy for three hours during the day when it serves as the commuting hub between Ouranopolis and Karyes, the capital of Athos, and the monasteries at the southern part of the peninsula. The pilgrims started taking off in different directions. Many took the bus to Karyes with the intention to go to the other side of the peninsula. I sat on a bar at Dafni observing the activity around while waiting for the other ferry to take me further south.

The village has all the characteristics of a tiny fishing village and consists of a post office and some souvenir shops. I saw a huge line of departing pilgrims entering the customs station to have their baggage inspected to impede the smuggling of the many treasures existing in the monasteries. There were also many police guards all around.

"Although this scenery does not look Byzantine at all, my impression is that I have crossed the border with Greece," I thought.

4

A SENSE OF ETERNITY

Simonos Petras Monastery

I took the *Agia Anna* ferry to my first destination, the monastery of Simonopetra. I was left with three other pilgrims at the quay. I looked up and saw, 300 meters above, a seven-story building surrounded by numerous balconies and terraces, perched on the cliffs. When I looked at the ascending trail, I saw the blond man, probably a foreigner like me, with a body shaped like a wrestler, disappearing on the ascending path propelled by his powerful muscles. The other two were Greeks around their forties, in no great physical condition, carrying a heavy bag and moving like turtles. I decided to take my own pace enjoying the peaceful envelope created by the savage mountain scenery precipitating into the sea. An inner voice said, "You will like it" and I replied, "By God, yes, I will like it!"

Along the ascending path I could see Simonopetra sprouting from a pinnacle. The monastery as built in 14th century and named after its founder, Saint Simon, who was moved to build a monastery over the sheer pinnacle that could be seen from his hut. Simonopetra is one of the most vigorous communities on Athos, with more than 50 monks from different countries.

Along the steep trail calm and peacefulness met me. The silence was interrupted only by the crickets along the way saying all the time, "Tune, tune, tune." When I finally arrived at Simonopetra, I was received by the guest master who offered the traditional welcome: water, *loukoumi* (sweet delight), and a cup of Greek coffee. The monasteries uphold a long tradition of hospitality. Food and a bed to sleep in are provided entirely free although the conditions are basic and pilgrims are supposed to rotate between the monasteries during their stay.

The blond man was already there. He was a Swiss who had been a policeman in the past and later on became a professor of history and comparative religions. I asked him why he decided to come to Athos.

"I live in Switzerland, my wife is Greek, and every year we come to Greece on vacation," he explained. "I left her with my two kids at Ouranopolis and came for one day to see what Athos is about and why so many people are devoting their entire lives for prayer and contemplation without access to the secular world. Also Orthodoxy is deeply rooted in early Christianity and this visit may offer some insights into my research of religions."

"I believe you are right," I commented. "Being a Roman Catholic, I find it very interesting to observe the differences between the two churches that once were one."

At that moment the guest master came and started explaining to us about the daily schedule at the monastery. "In keeping with biblical tradition, the church's day begins in the evening. The biblical account of the days of creation mentions the evening first: 'And the evening and the morning were the first day' (Gen. 1:5); therefore the first service of the church day is Vespers, the evening service, sung towards the end of afternoon (around 17:00hs) when the faithful give thanks to the Lord for the past day and ask his grace for the coming evening. It is followed by dinner (18:30hs) and then a period of relaxation. At sunset all the monks retire to their cells and the gates of the monastery are closed. The period between sunset and sunrise is dedicated exclusively to rest, silence, and prayer.

"This is a reminder of how the idea of time in antiquity differed from ours. Indeed the present system of dividing day and night into 24 hours of equal length was not employed in civil life until the 14th century although it had already been used by astronomers. Previously it was the general custom to divide each of the periods of light and darkness, which along the year vary in length, into an equal number of 12 hours. Strange as this may now seem, we must remember that in ancient times most human activities took place during daylight, a way of living still maintained in Athos.

"The most important of all the divine services is the Divine Liturgy, which is usually celebrated before sunrise. The morning office begins before sunrise (4:00hs) and lasts about three and a half hours. Pilgrims are expected to check out before 9:00hs."

He motioned with a sweep of his arm around the periphery of the grounds. "Please feel free to walk around, but keep in mind that the gates will close right after sunset."

The guest master took us to our rooms to rest. At 15:45hs the hollow beat of the traditional symantron (a long wooden plank hit by a mallet and used, instead of a bell, to summon monks and pilgrims to prayer) filled the courtyard, inviting everybody to church. I slowly crossed the interior of the monastery that reminded me of a medieval castle and arrived at church, where I was invited to take a seat. The church was illuminated only by the twinkling sunlight entering by the small windows while a choir was singing plaintive chanting with the monks constantly repeating, *"Kyrie eleison"* (Lord Jesus Christ, have mercy on me). I was surrounded by Byzantine art, Byzantine music, and Byzantine spirituality. I was back in time to the Byzantine Empire.

Mount Athos

After the liturgy the abbot led everybody to the refectory for the evening meal. We ate with the monks at the same refectory but at different tables. I was curious and observant of everything during my first meal in Athos. They served bread, olives, vegetables, rice, pasta, and fruit. The abbot, sitting at the main table, rang a bell and everybody started eating in silence and at great speed. "Why such a hurry if we have plenty of time?" I wondered. During the meal a monk read a prayer from the Bible. After 10 minutes the abbot rang the bell again and everybody stopped eating.

"These guys have not learned yet how to taste and savor the food. Worst of all, they do not know the basic rule of digestion:

to eat slowly and to chew as much as they can," I thought with some irritation because I had missed the beautiful peaches offered for dessert.

From the refectory we were taken to the chapel again, where a monk presented the monastery's relics. He explained to us that the veneration of bodily remains from saints is a practice dating to the early church. One of the ways of evaluating the status of a monastery is by the relics it has. Since antiquity it is believed that a power resides in a saint's bodily remains that is capable of initiating miracles for those faithful who come close to them. The righteous soul which dwelled for so many years in the body of the saint, although not present any more, has left a great force residing in the relics. It is not by chance that Rome has been a major peregrination center for millennia since there one will find the relics of the two greatest apostles of Christianity, St. Peter and St. Paul.

In Athos all the monasteries have priceless treasures from their Byzantine past. Treasures of particular religious significance such as relics of the saints and miracle-working icons are often kept in church and displayed for veneration by the pilgrims. For each relic shown the Orthodox gave the sign of the cross three times and at the end as in the beginning they kissed the many icons around the church.

After the relics veneration I took the free time to interact with other pilgrims. Commenting with the Swiss about the eating speed at the refectory, he clarified the reason for me. "Monastics are imitators of Christ. Like Christ they fast and they live a life of poverty. Since gluttony has always been considered a major vice, they are careful not to eat that which brings temptation or creates attachment to food. The monk's life is one of service not of pleasure and the meal is only to provide sustenance for his bodily needs. That is why they eat so fast."

The Greek men I left on the ascending path were sharing a room with me. They explained that they go every year to Athos and their heavy bag contained many bottles of raki, a strong Greek spirit, to drink every evening. It seemed like they were coming to Athos to enjoy a "spiritual vacation" with some of the pleasures of the secular world included.

"The motivations for coming to Athos are very different for each pilgrim," I thought.

We all went to bed early and at 3:30hs the sound of the symantron awakened us so that we could flock to Divine Liturgy. This was a truly unique experience. The church was dimly lit by candles and by the oil lamps in front of the icons and Byzantine wall frescoes. The monks, with their long beards and black cassocks, were dark shadows shuffling around, each one knowing exactly the role to be played during the church service. The chanting was pure harmony and the myrrh incensed the air, adding to the mysticism of the occasion.

Around 7:00hs, at the end of the liturgy, the Swiss and I were invited by Pater Macarios to join him at the guest house while another monk took care of the Greek pilgrims. Pater Macarios, a French Catholic by origin, explained that he had been in Orthodox monastic life 25 years. After knowing that we were not Orthodox, he started explaining some of the fundamentals of the Orthodox Church. "The unity of the early Christian Church has been fragmented along the centuries in three main stages. The first separation occurred in the 5th and 6th centuries when what is known today as the Oriental Orthodox churches (presently Iran and Iraq, Syria, Ethiopia, Egypt, and Armenia) split from the main body. The second separation in 1054 disunited the main body of Christians into two communions: in Western Europe, the Roman Catholic Church, and in the Byzantine Empire, the Orthodox Church. Finally the third main separation was in the 16th century between the Roman Catholic Church and the Protestants."

Offering us a glass of water, he went on, "The Orthodox faith, different from Roman Catholicism, is a family of self-governing churches, organized by patriarchates, which are held together by unity in the faith and communion in the sacraments, and are located in four geographic areas. First there are the Orthodox who live in the eastern Mediterranean (where are located the four ancient patriarchates of Constantinople, Alexandria, Antioch, and Jerusalem) as a minority in a society predominantly Muslin. Secondly there are the Orthodox Churches of Cyprus and Greece, in which is still very present the church-state alliance like in the old days of the Byzantine Empire. After the fall of Constantinople the Orthodox Church became a civil as well as a religious institution and the patriarch was recognized as the secular and spiritual head of the Greek nation by the Ottoman rulers. This situation continued until the formation of the Greek state in 1923 and in Cyprus until the death of Archbishop Makarios III, also the head of the state, in 1977. Thirdly there are the Orthodox churches in eastern Europe comprising Russia, Serbia, Romania, Bulgaria, Georgia, and Albania, accounting for over 85 percent of the total of the Orthodox. Finally there are the Orthodox communities of the diasporas, formed mainly of immigrants and their descendants.

"Another important difference between Catholicism and Orthodoxy is that the latter maintained tradition. A distinctive characteristic of our Church is its sense of living continuity with the Church of ancient times, which is summoned up in the word *tradition,* which means 'the transmission of knowledge' by previous Fathers, generation after generation, since the beginning of Christianity."

"Could you tell us a bit about what it means to be a monk?" I asked Pater Macarios.

He nodded, "In the monasteries of Athos, our personal and community lives are regulated on a daily basis into four sectors: a common worship spent in church; private prayer and study in the cell; work; and rest, devoted to sleep and other personal occupations. None of these periods is continuous. Uninterrupted continuity is sought only in mental prayer to be maintained through all sectors of life. The monk, in constant motion, should become a whole faculty of perception, constantly being recreated to attain a state of peace, calm, and inactivity with the aim at some point of being united with God. Counting the knots of our prayer rope, we continuously repeat, *'Kyrie eleison,'* to concelebrate in harmony with the Lord.

"The church dominates the space of a monastery and marks its spiritual identity. The beginning and the end of monastic life are the worship of God. Worship and prayers have the goal of subjugating the passions and cultivating the virtues. With these objectives in mind we have no access to TV, radio, newspapers, and periodicals. Our focus is the spiritual world. A monastery, like a garden, is a burial ground of dead seeds from which new life blossoms."

"Oh, oh, this is a recurrent theme since the Mysteries of Eleusis," I thought. But without being provocative, I continued with my questions to understand more about Athos. I asked him, "But are all the monks living at monasteries?"

"In addition to the ruling monasteries there are 12 sketes in Athos, similar to the monasteries but much smaller. After the sketes come the cells, looking very much like farmhouses, housing three to four monks. Then there are the small houses for a single monk and finally the true hermitages, simple huts or more often just caves in the cliffs. Many of these cluster around the southern tip of the peninsula called the desert of Athos. There men, a number of whom over alarming precipices accessible only by decaying ladders spend their lives in prayer and are rarely seen. Although all these additional types of organizations are under the authority of 1 of the 20 monasteries, they are not maintained by them and have the obligation to find ways to sustain themselves."

It was almost 9:00hs and Pater Macarios was getting tired since he had to rest a while before getting to his daily activities. The Swiss then shot a series of questions at him, probably afraid of not having his questions answered, "Is it worthwhile to be a monk? How can you deal with chastity? Don't you get bored doing the same things every day?"

Very calmly the Father answered the questions, "I do not regret at all my decision to become a monk. Although in the beginning it was very difficult and full of temptations, with perseverance and faith my path gradually unfolded the beauty and simplicity of the Divine itself. A major issue along this route is the control of the passions, which need to be dealt with by obedience to a set of rules.

"Chastity is among these rules and you deal with it like when you decide to quit smoking. You demonstrate to your body that you are in control and not the other way around. Also as part of these rules is the organization of your daily routine. Judging from the outside, it seems like you are 'executing the same things every day' because the real transformation is occurring inside you. What is really happening is that the control of the passions associated with a daily schedule and uninterrupted prayer creates another dimension of time, a sense of eternity you cannot perceive while living in the secular world."

We left the monastery to go to Dafni. The Swiss was returning to Ouranopolis and I took the bus to Karyes, the administrative center of the monastic republic. The village is situated in the middle of the peninsula with 200 residents. From there I started walking, in a forest of walnut and hazel trees, the descending path to the Monastery of Iviron. I kept reflecting about the experience and the teachings of Pater Macarios and what motivates monks to devote their whole lives for such a strict schedule. This is not an easy answer, especially if you do not experience what they experience, but coming from the secular world, I have to admit that this requires a lot of sense of vocation and dedication.

"But it is quite an experience to interact with them," I thought. "*Axion Esti*," I said to myself in the midst of the thick vegetation and running waters leading to Iviron.

29

5

INTERNALS AND EXTERNALS

Iviron, founded in 980 AD, sits by the sea and is surrounded by cultivated land. I went straight to the guest house, where I was offered water, olives, bread, cucumber, and fruit. "What a banquet," I thought.

Daily schedules were similar to the ones at Simonopetra. There I met Father Sinesios, who was particularly welcoming with the pilgrims. He was a middle-aged monk, full of energy, and had the look of someone for whom all those routines and methods had produced calm, peace, wisdom, and love to be shared with others. He started showing us the two churches of the monastery. The main church is one of the largest in Athos, with an 11th-century mosaic floor, an impressive chandelier, and two Hellenistic columns with ram's head capitals from a Poseidon temple which once stood there.

He explained to us, "With the proclamation of religious freedom by Emperor Constantine in 313, Christianity grew in power until it became the religion of the empire. As a cost effective way of quickly penetrating into society and at the same time erasing the memory of other cults, Christian temples appropriated styles from the existing pagan temples. Just as an example, the Parthenon on the Acropolis in Athens was transformed into a basilica and in the 12th century it was used as the cathedral of Athens. As the temples were erected, the need also arose for an architectural and artistic expression that could embody the triumph of the new religion. Even old words acquired new meaning. In ancient Greece and Rome *ekklesia* implied the assembly of all adult male citizens, those entitled to participate in political life. This word came into Christianity to denote the church or the place where the faithful assembled to worship God.

"The Christian temple is the place of union between heaven and earth, the divine and the human. Initially church temples, following the existing pagans, appeared in two basic types: one circular and centralized, the other rectangular and elongated. Each type conveyed a different way of approaching the divine. In the circular temples the point of union was at its center; in the rectangular ones the altar was approached after the faithful crossed the temple, which served as a sacred way."

Father Sinesios led us to the back of the monastery, elucidating us as we walked. "The round temples were designed initially as tomb-shrines of martyrs and as baptisteries. The best preserved circular church is the Pantheon in Rome, with the largest dome ever built, which inspired later domes including Hagia Sofia in Constantinople and Michelangelo's St. Peter's in Rome. The rectangular type, known as basilica, has an entrance from the west for the faithful to walk towards and facing the eastern end, marked by the apse sanctuary. In the centralized buildings the longitudinal axis of the basilicas was replaced by a vertical axis rising above the point which was the focus of the building's function. The combination of the two axes led to a new architectural form, the domed basilica. Later on, other architectural forms appeared such as the inscribed-cross type with dome, of which many examples are still preserved in Greece, and the Russian style with its distinctive cupola, which resembles the flame of a candle."

Someone from our group asked if the Byzantine architecture included symbolism and Father Sinesios replied, "The architecture and decoration of a Byzantine church are a reflection of cosmological beliefs. It is an architecture of interiors, which is accentuated with the development of the inscribed-cross with dome plan that created a series of niches and vaults decorated according to a strict iconography in order to orient the faithful.

"It is a reminder of the prosperous interior to be constructed inside each of us. The building is dominated by a dome, symbol of heaven; the walls are covered with frescoes or mosaic representations, an artistic vision that mirrors the hierarchy governing the universe. At various places in the church icons are positioned. They are the main means by which the faithful communicate with God. The paintings at a Byzantine church gave visual expression to the fundamental beliefs of Orthodoxy and served as the 'Bible of the illiterate' since even the uneducated could grasp the visual Christian teachings around the temple.

"The main area of the church is called the nave, which means "ship," to remind us that we are a community of believers journeying towards God as on the deck of a ship. As long as we are on board, we will be safe from the stormy seas that are always threatening us. The number of cupolas on a church has its own significance. A single cupola honors the One God; three, the Holy Trinity; five, Christ and his four evangelists. Moreover the bell tower located over the entrance is important. The sound of the bells is not simply a gong that summons people to church. It is a melody that spiritually permeates the environs of the church, serving as a reminder to pray for those who are immersed in the activities of everyday life. However what you will normally hear in Athos is the symantron. The bells are left for the festive days. And this afternoon when you hear the symantron, do not forget to answer the call and come to liturgy."

After the thorough explanation about Byzantine architecture and its symbology, Father Sinesios took us to the other church which houses the miraculous icon of the Portaitissa ("She Who Guards the Gate"), the monastery's pride. It is said that great disasters will visit Athos if she ever leaves the mountain. He continued with his lecture, now explaining about the place assigned to icons in Orthodoxy.

"Icon painting, Byzantine music, incense preparation, making Church vestments, and translating or writing spiritual books are all arts that originated in Byzantium and are executed in the monasteries as part of the daily monastic routine. Athos's iconography is certainly the most well known. Byzantine iconography is one of the basic ways for someone to approach God. The images on icons must conform to the iconographic tradition, which has been worked out over the centuries. A newly painted icon should always be blessed in church and sprinkled with holy water. Icons are part of tradition and as religious art they reflect not only the aesthetic sentiments of the artist but the mind of the Church since they are designed to arouse appropriate emotions in the beholder. They convey in images what the sacred scriptures describe in words. Icons are constantly venerated by the Orthodox faithful. An Orthodox prostrates himself before these icons, kisses them, and burns candles in front of them. When they pray before an icon, they are not praying to the material of which it is made but to the Lord, the Mother of God, and the saints who are depicted on it."

He left us in the church so we could fully appreciate the icons and the church's interior and navigate towards the transcendent.

After Vespers I did not miss the opportunity to meet him in the courtyard. "Father Sinesios," I said, "I greatly enjoyed your introduction to the symbols of the church, but what impressed me most was how you were transmitting that to us. I could feel that you had lots of pleasure in doing that."

He laughed and replied, "Before I came to Iviron, I was a surgeon. When I was accepted by the monastery, they used my skills for peeling potatoes as part of my daily routines. Looking back to those days now, I understand that the abbot did not want to transplant someone from the secular world to the monastery and keep him performing the same things he was used to. Peeling potatoes was a way for me to understand that I was living in a community and that my skills could help my inner development. However first I needed to obey the monastery's rules and guidance. I needed to understand that work is itself a prayerful activity with the goal of overcoming our rebellious nature and keeping us in transformational motion. Monastic life involves a system called by psychologists 'feedback loop.' Giving attention to externals, we improve our internal state, which in turn will affect the externals. When I realized that peeling potatoes was helping the sustenance of our monastic community, I felt so good internally that this affected the way I was working in the kitchen. You may be doing a simple task, but if you realize that which is your humble part, on the whole you will do it with greater pleasure and attention. Internals and externals interact with one another in an endless process that renovates each one of us.

"Presently receiving pilgrims is part of my daily tasks. And I am conscious that sharing with you some of the symbolisms of the church is a way of facilitating your introspection, reflection, and prayer. Ultimately I will be contributing to your spiritual development. During early Christianity and later on, illiteracy was the norm and the teachings of the faith were brought to the believers by the word of mouth, stories, symbols, and images. Once you understand the message conveyed by the symbols, you change the way you look at them and you begin feeling that you belong to an uninterrupted chain of devotion and spirituality. You feel a part of 2,000 years of continuity, which although a drop in the ocean of eternity is a lot more than the minutes and seconds pressuring our secular daily lives."

"But don't you think that all these ways of connecting believers to God are sort of unnecessary?" I asked tentatively. "Can't you just get the same results by simply praying directly to God without icons, music, symbols, etc.?"

Father Sinesios smiled patiently. "What you are saying many others before you have said already. Iconography, for example, was a discussion in early Christianity that lasted 120 years. In 726 AD the Byzantine emperor Leo III began attacking icons because he saw in all images a latent idolatry. The controversy continued until 843 AD when the Byzantine empress Theodora finally reinstated permanently the use of icons in church. Since then they are honored with the same veneration as shown to other material symbols such as the cross and the Bible. Icons are part of the teachings of the Church.

"All the fundamental wisdom present in the Orthodox Church today is based on the first seven councils of Christians, which were held between 325 and 787 AD. All these councils had their origin in a particular crisis of the Church. They were Greek-speaking and held in Eastern Europe or Asia Minor. The Orthodox Church sees this period as next to the Bible and the great age of theology.

"The seven councils articulated and defined the fundamental doctrines and have served as our fundamental guidelines since then. This does not mean that doctrine is encapsulating everything. There is a lot of space for flexibility to be given to the way each individual pursues his own path. At Iviron, for example, like in other monasteries, we live in a community. But hermits prefer to live alone in huts although we share the same faith."

"Are there still many hermits?" I asked in wonder.

"Oh yes, since the third century AD! By that time Christians started adopting ascetic forms of self-discipline, seeking religious insight through solitude and ecstatic experience. First they inhabited the desert lands of Egypt, Syria, and Asia Minor, seeking closeness to God. They were known first as 'hermits' (a person from the desert), then as 'anchorites' (he who has withdrawn from the world for religious reasons), and later on as 'ascetics' (rigorously self-disciplined, one who exercises), and finally as 'monks' (the solitary or single one). The leading hermits became known as the 'Desert Fathers' and that is the reason why the southern part of Athos, with higher concentration of them, is known as the desert of Athos."

"But in what sense is it characteristic of following Christ to flee to the desert?" I frowned.

"The answer to this may be found in considering Christ's own departures to the desert, which is a type of place where the human heart is in a state of aloneness, in a state to meditate, to pray, to fast, to reflect upon one's inner existence and one's relationship to the ultimate reality, God."

"But the desert life is not for everyone," I protested in self-defense. "The demands of ascetic life are beyond the courage of many Christians."

Turning toward his room for the night, Father Sinesios agreed. "You are right. For many, a more moderated form of withdrawal and seclusion is more suitable. During the fourth century AD there was a gradual move away from solitary monasticism towards a communal life. This development was very helpful in curbing most of the extremes and eccentricities from the early anchorites. It also reintroduced a key element into Christian life, which is the sanctifying effect of having to live in proximity to others. As you can see, there are many ways leading to the same end and you do not need to face your journey alone because the labyrinth is well known in all of its extension. You have only to believe and choose your way. And at the end of the path where you would expect to be alone, you will be together with all those who crossed it before you."

The following day I left Iviron for the monastery of Stavronikita. The path was by the sea. I passed by a cell and then a skete. These small communal organizations are not very receptive to pilgrims unless you have been invited by one of their monks. Some signs close to the skete insinuated for pilgrims to keep away from them and clearly indicated the way to Stavronikita.

"Well, this is implied anyway in the definition of who a monk is, a solitary one, one who withdraws from the world," I told myself.

Far from the secular world, in motion towards the monastery of Stavronikita, I was overwhelmed by the amount of wisdom and information I had received in just two days. I could feel that all those externals were beginning to permeate me. Wisdom was constantly dripping inside myself and beginning to decorate my interior. *"Axion Esti,"* I said to myself.

6

BELIEVE AND YOU
WILL FIND IT

Stavronikita, founded in 1536, is the smallest and youngest monastery in Athos. Stavronikita is essentially a cozy fortified tower. When I arrived, the monks were still resting before the beginning of their daily work.

I was received by Andreas, a dokimos (novice), the name given for those who are trying to become monks. I asked dokimos Andreas how he decided to become a monk.

He readily answered, "I started visiting Athos more and more and developed an affinity for Stavronikita. One day a monk to whom I was always close asked me if I wanted to be a monk. I was prepared for that question and from that point on he took care of making me certain of my decision and guiding me through all of its consequences to me and to my beloved ones. A very difficult moment was when I left home. I knew it would be hard leaving the family, telling them my decision later on, and letting the Virgin Mary guide all those involved in this difficult transition."

"Will it take you very long to become a monk?" I asked him.

He shrugged. "I have been a dokimos for the past six months. Only when the dokimos feels he is ready and the abbot agrees, he is ordained and is allowed to wear the monastic gown and hat. This is a process that may take a year or more, during which the dokimos is tested about his decision. From the moment he is ordained as a monk, he confirms that he intends to continue in the monastic state and to abide by the rules of the monastery by taking the vows of stability, obedience, poverty, and chastity. He begins to use a belt as the symbol of chastity, continence, and chosen restriction from liberty. He has now died to the outside world and has been reborn into the holy world of Mount Athos. He gives up his past life, his name, his status and property. He takes up the name of one of the saints with the same initial as his original name. Instead of a surname he uses the name of his monastery. As you can comprehend, the decision to become a monk affects not only you, your family, and your friends but also the community in which the new monk will be living."

"And it is a decision with no return, for the whole life," I added.

"Indeed it is," he replied. "However a whole life is nothing if compared with the unimaginable magnitude of eternity. This is, at the very end, a decision affecting this ephemeral life in return for the good consequences during the eternal one."

Stavronikita has a slightly different routine from the two other monasteries I had visited. The main meal is served around noon and only after pilgrims are taken to the dormitories. Since I arrived early, there was plenty of time to mingle with others. After a while Father Panayotis joined us. He was young, talkative, and very patient indeed. While I stayed with the others at the veranda, close to the guest house, he opened the church five times for the pilgrims passing by to venerate the holy icons inside. I commented on this to him and he replied, "Pilgrimage means different things to different people. The Greek word for pilgrimage is *proskynesis,* which means 'prostration or veneration.' Originally *proskynesis* was the Persian custom of genuflection before their king or their god. Persians believed that their kings were direct descendants from god. Greeks too believed that their kings were descendants from their Olympian gods but treated them as equals, reserving acts of prostration for only when in front of their gods' images. In other words the act of *proskynesis* stresses what you do when you arrive rather than on how you got there. Therefore I cannot obstruct anyone who is on his quest for the renewal of his soul with the simultaneous movement of his feet. Everyone has the right to venerate the holy icons and move on."

I arrived early for the evening services. Monks and pilgrims appeared, and one by one, repeatedly made the sign of the cross when they entered the church and in front the icons. Father Panayotis explained to me the importance of this symbolic gesture.

"Christian veneration of the cross goes back to the first century AD. By the second and third centuries the veneration of the cross had become so widespread among Christians that pagans called them 'cross-worshippers.' During the beginning of the fourth century Emperor Constantine, while still a pagan, received a revelation from heaven that if he placed the sign of the cross on the standards of his army, he would win a decisive battle at the Milvio bridge in Rome. He defeated Emperor Maxentius, who had a much larger army, and that was the turning point not only for the reunification of the Roman Empire but more importantly for Christianity. From a persecuted religion, with lots of martyrs used as entertainment for the Roman crowds at the Coliseum, the Christian faith gained strength across the Roman Empire. From that time on churches were decorated with crosses both inside and out.

"The sign of the cross became the symbol to express the inner belief of the faithful. To make the sign of the cross properly the fingers of the right hand are brought together so that the ends of the first three fingers (the thumb, the index and middle fingers) are joined together, representing the Holy Trinity while the remaining two fingers (the ring finger and the little finger) are folded into the palm of the hand, symbolizing the two natures, divine and human, of Jesus Christ."

He demonstrated the gesture and continued, "In making the sign of the cross, we place the three joined fingers on the forehead, to sanctify the mind; on the belly to sanctify our inmost feelings; and then on the right and left shoulders, to strengthen our spiritual and physical faculties. This is made three times over the four points of the cross, creating the power of the numbers 7 (3+4) and 12 (3*4)."

"What do you mean by the power of 7 and 12?" I immediately asked.

"Ancient civilizations have always recognized the 7 as sacred, representing the cosmos and its perfection. The number 7 is also associated with the rhythms of the human life. The embryo develops for seven weeks before becoming a fetus and then the birth of the child will be after seven new moons. The Old Testament uses seven names to refer to earth and another seven for the cosmos. And according to the Apocalypse, which is the vision the apostle John had at the island of Patmos, not far from here, the end of the world will be announced by the breaking of the seven seals, followed by the sound of seven trumpets played by seven angels.

"While the number 7 is associated with steps to virtue and wisdom, the number 12 brings the completion of cycles. It is not a coincidence that the year is divided into 12 months. Twelve complete lunar cycles are equivalent to a year. Twelve and their multiples are all over the Bible's Apocalypse. The faithful at the end of time will number 144,000, 12,000 from each of the 12 tribes of Israel (Apoc. 7); the walls of Jerusalem had 12 foundations and on them there were the names of the 12 apostles (Apoc. 21); the Holy City, the New Jerusalem, was measured by an angel and was 12,000 stadia in length (Apoc. 21); and the wall was 144 cubits thick with 12 gates (Apoc. 21).

"The symbol of the cross is said to symbolize crossroads, that place in which all things converge and from which all things diverge in a multitude of possibilities. The sign of the cross drawing upon us the power of the 7 and 12 means that we are not only thanking God for the wisdom, perfection, and beauty of human life (the power of 7) but also driving away all the evil influences which comes from the demons that will tempt us in all the crossroads of our lives until the end of time (the power of 12)."

After Vespers I went to bed reflecting on what a symbolic and mystical world Athos is. Imagine 1,000 years ago—no electrical lights, no cell phones, no television, no newspapers to read. Residents were completely surrounded by nature and living according to the daily cycles of day and night, admiring the stars each night, with the succession of seasons during the year determining the rhythm of their lives. Also the great majority of the people could not read, information traveled through the roads of the Roman Empire with the speed of foot or horse, and all tradition was conveyed through stories told generation after generation or by symbols present in art. Church was powerful. The Church of the Byzantine Empire and its people were expecting the second coming of the Messiah and the end of time. Imagine the faith and the fear of those people, having heard the Apocalypse told by the priest and immediately after, how they would feel doing the sign of the cross three times. Those were the feelings that were flourishing in me. I was becoming enthusiastic, which comes from the Greek word *enthousiasmos,* meaning 'to be possessed by God' or in other words I felt that I was beginning to transcend the secular world and to be immersed in the world of Athos.

The next day I woke up with the sound of the symantron and hurried to the Divine Liturgy. It lasted more than four hours since it was a Sunday, but I did not feel it was so long. Some people are probably held back from a fearless participation because they are afraid of their ignorance. But if you know that you know what is going on, you can perhaps dare to participate and adore it. Knowledge and love go hand in hand. That was probably what was happening to me. As Father Sinesios from Iviron said, "The more you understand about the symbols around, the more your introspection, reflection, and prayers are facilitated."

I said good-bye to Father Panayotis and took the coastal trail to the monastery of Pantokratoros from where I boarded the midday boat to Great Lavra. It had no resemblance to the ferries I had used on the western side of the peninsula. It was more like one of those many colorful fishing boats seen around Greece with space for no more than 20 pilgrims. By my side was a Greek whom when I asked what he did for a living simply replied, "I think."

"But what do you mean by that?" I asked. "After all we all think."

"You may be right," he replied, "but there are many levels of thinking and mine is of the highest caliber. I study and teach philosophy."

"This is going to be a tough conversation. I had better keep my mouth shut," I thought.

When he asked me what I was doing in Athos, I gave my usual answer, not very interested in moving the conversation forward. Just as a matter of courtesy I also asked if he was on a pilgrimage and he replied, "No, no. The Aegean is my home and I always travel around to research about the great philosophers and their legacy. I am going to Lavra to delve into some manuscripts written by Patriarch Photius, who revived the study of Plato during the ninth century."

"But what has Christianity to do with pagan philosophers?" I asked.

"This same question was also asked by Tertulian, a Christian writer. He asked, 'What does Athens have to do with Jerusalem?' The two major strands of Western tradition, the classical Greek world of Plato and Aristotle and the biblical world of Moses and Jesus, came together in the writings of the Church. The synthesis of faith and reason, theology and philosophy, were fundamental to the understanding, development, and spread of Christian teachings.

"Some of the differences between the modern and the ancient world are illusory. Central to ancient Greek religion was sacrifice. Sacrifices were conducted in the ritualized context of a religious festival. Animals were slaughtered on an altar to honor the gods, and in front of the whole community. According to the writings of our ancestors, the gods enjoyed the smoke of the burning meat and fat. Any resemblance to churches being incensed and the smoke going up to the heavens?" he grinned.

"The ritual of sacrificing an animal created a victim which took all the sins of the community. After the sacrifice the 'scapegoat' was dismembered, barbecued, and eaten by the faithful for the expiation of the guilt of the worshippers."

"But this is the liturgy of the Christian church in which Christ, the lamb, was sacrificed for our salvation. And also during the communion the faithful take His dismembered body....," I protested.

"Exactly, this is the point I want to make. In the Orthodox Church the liturgy is very similar to paganism since during communion the faithful receive bread and wine as the flesh and blood of Christ. And if you are in Greece on Easter Sunday, you will see a huge picnic scene when families gather together to barbecue a lamb. Probably they are not aware that they are reenacting the ancient ritual of sacrifice.

"This synthesis between paganism and Christianity has to be credited to Emperor Constantine, who legalized the Christian faith in 313 AD. There were several religions across the Roman Empire and he, as a good politician, saw the emergence of an official cult, closely controlled by the emperor, as a way of having more influence over the spiritual power. In 324 he became the sole Roman emperor and one year later, losing his patience with the conflicts in the Church, he convened the First Ecumenical Council of Nicea (today's Iznik in Turkey). He told the 318 bishops who took part in it to formulate a consistent doctrine that would be universal, i.e., catholic, and that could be understood and practiced by all. Meanwhile the emperor remained personally converted to the Mithraic sun cult. He commanded the Christians to hold their services every Sunday (the day of the sun) and their Nativity feast on December 25. According to the Mithraic cult, that date, the winter solstice, was the nativity of the sun when the longest night of the year brings in it the seeds of longer days, a growing light, meaning the rebirth of the winter sun."

We turned to admire the scenery we were passing. The philosopher continued, "There are many pagan precursors to Christian rites. A Lent of 40 days, for example, was observed by the worshippers of the great Babylonian goddess Ishtar as a preliminary to the great annual spring festivals. Some insist that the rites of Easter in Greece bear a striking resemblance to those evolved in the cult of Adonis (*Adon* meaning 'god' in Semitic languages), who died a violent death and returned to life.

"And if you think that the monks in Athos are the only ascetics, in the fourth century BC, centuries before Athos existed, Zeno, a member of Plato's Academy, created a philosophical tradition that began Stoicism. He taught his students to keep the body's cravings in check so that the mind could be free to contemplate higher realities. St. Paul, well-versed in Greek thought and a fluent speaker of the language, used Stoic notions such as asceticism, humility, harmony, and the brotherhood of man in addressing the Athenians. In a nutshell the Christians felt that the cult of reason they had inherited from the Greeks was invaluable for spreading their message."

I interrupted, "And I thought that the great example of ancient religions transitioning into Christianity was the Mysteries of Eleusis."

"This is one of many. Greek influences on Christianity were pervasive not only in liturgy and borrowing from mystery religions, but also in dogma, ethics, and symbolism. The crossover line between the pre-Christian and Christian traditions is often an ambiguous one.

"With relation to the pagan philosophers, Christian intellectuals turned to Platonic thinking to expound their faith and to make the Christian doctrine appealing to educated classes and to explain and elucidate who Jesus was. Origen, for example, was recognized as a brilliant Christian scholar although he was also accused of combining the Gospels with too much pagan philosophy. He claimed that with the tools of reason as perfected by the Greek philosophers, one could arrive at the truth found in scripture. He combined Christian faith with Platonic thought to explain the Trinity, which was approved as a dogma at the First Ecumenical Council. His denial of carnal resurrection led to his posthumous condemnation in 553 AD by the Council of Constantinople.

"Curiously, at some monasteries such as Vatopedi, one finds wall paintings of Socrates and Plato incorporating them into their own conception of 'Greek-Christian' culture. Christian theology has turned to Plato and the thinkers formed at his Academy to explain and elucidate who Jesus was."

"I saw in Athens the old city gate leading to the Academy," I commented. "Unfortunately we can see no remains from the Academy except the gardens."

The philosopher nodded. "Plato's Academy flourished for 900 years until 529 AD when it was closed down by the Emperor Justinian with a special edict saying that 'henceforth never again shall there be anyone to lecture on philosophy or explain the laws in Athens' on the basis that it was a pagan establishment. However the Academy survived this attack.

"Interestingly Plato (429-347 BC) was convinced that the origin or first principle of all things must be One, a Creator who endows the world with intelligible order by applying forms to an equally pre-existing matter. The One is above knowledge and understanding and hence is incomprehensible. We cannot have a view of the One, only union with it. This union is possible because the One is the source of all being and all being returns to it, like coming home, a return to where the being has always been although the journey is always long and difficult. As you can understand, his ideas were not so pagan after all."

The philosopher waited for my comment and when I remained silent, he went on, "Byzantium was the heir and guardian of Plato's legacy. After Constantinople's fall to the Fourth Crusade (mostly composed of Franks) in 1204, a disaster which led to the partition of the Byzantine Empire, anarchy reigned as Greeks and Franks battled for dominion. The incessant ethnic strife would weaken Byzantium, heralding the final downfall of Constantinople to the Ottomans.

"The Greeks controlled the Peloponnese and in 1249 founded on its southern part the walled town of Mystras, which turned it into one of Byzantium's last spiritual and artistic centers, drawing thinkers and artists from Constantinople and the West.

"Mystras's most illustrious figure was Plethon, an ardent admirer and follower of Plato's ideas. In 1438 AD Plethon accompanied Emperor John Palaeologos and Patriarch Josef to the Council of Florence-Ferrara, convened to examine the possibility of reuniting the Eastern and Western Churches. In Florence he convinced the local ruler, Cosimo dei Medici, to found an academy for the study of Plato.

"The entire corpus of Greek philosophy and scientific knowledge was passed on to the Arabs during the seventh century AC after they conquered Egypt and Alexandria in particular, home of the famous library where Eratosthenes, chief librarian in the third century BC, proved the Earth a sphere and accurately measured its circumference. The Arabs took many books with them and made considerable contributions to the wisdom they found. Eventually this knowledge returned to Byzantium and migrated to the West. The new academy created by Cosimo dei Medici was pivotal in this course. The academy revived interest in Plato, forgotten in Western Europe. (A professor in the academy would later be Galileo Galilei.) The classical Hellenic inheritance was then transmitted to the West by the translation of Greek texts into Latin, creating the foundations of the philosophical revival during the Italian Renaissance."

'The more I travel, the more I learn," I mused. "Would it be a coincidence that I am coming across the right persons or is it my deep inner desire for a self-renewal that is making all those encounters come true?" I asked myself.

Most likely, the old man in Ouranopolis was right when he said, "Believe and you will find it."

7

THE ECHOES OF THE LANDSCAPE

We disembarked at the Monastery of Great Lavra, which is built on the southeastern end of the Athos Peninsula. It is the oldest, the biggest, and the leading monastery. It was founded in 963 AD by Athanasios, who although from a very rich family entered the area as a peasant intending to lose his identity. The construction of the monumental monastery shocked some of the hermits, who perceived the aesthetic life as an escape to total solitude and a complete withdrawal from secular life. They accused Athanasios of bringing the outside world to Mount Athos and protested to the Byzantine emperor Ioannis Tsimiskis, who not only did not uphold the accusations but recognized and confirmed the rights of the big monasteries.

The monastery occupies the first rank in the hierarchical order and it is inhabited by more than 300 monks. So far the Great Lavra has produced more than 26 patriarchs and 150 bishops, giving some idea of its importance to Orthodoxy.

It features the shape of a small medieval town and is surrounded by a strong fortress with 15 towers. Inside and outside these towers are 37 chapels and more than 15 chapels in its enormous courtyard. The library contains more than 30,000 printed books and 2,000 manuscripts. Uniquely among the other monasteries, it has never been ravaged by fire.

Everything in Great Lavra makes you feel small—the size of the monastery, the number of monks around, the activity, and above all that the Holy Mountain rising nearby. After Vespers and before the closing of the monastery's gate, I sat on a bench outside. Vineyards were around me; I could feel the fragrance of a jasmine tree and hear the pulsating symphony of the crickets.

"Friends, as you all requested, I am tuning in very quickly," I said to them.

A gentle breeze was embracing me. All my senses were active and I was admiring the mountain piercing the sky. A monk came and sat by my side.

"This bench is my favorite spot," he said. "From here I have the best views of the mountain, which has a very special meaning for me."

"Why is that?" I asked.

"Before being a monk, my hobby was alpinism," he explained. "Fifteen years ago I decided to come to Athos and hike up to the mountain's summit. Once on top of the mountain I was awe-struck. There were no clouds in the sky and I could see the whole Aegean Sea. Paradoxically in front of that vast spectacle of the outer world I switched to my inner world and I was overcome by an inexpressible longing to grasp the essence of this landscape. As Lawrence Durrell has told us in a famous passage, 'The essential sense of landscape values is there. If you just close your eyes and breathe softly through your nose, you will hear the whispered message, for all landscapes ask the same question.' And that is what I did. Quietly within myself, I opened my ears to the whisper of the landscape and heard it saying, 'I am watching you. Are you watching yourself in me?' At that moment there was a fundamental turning point from the desire to see to the need to know myself. It was like the landscape was digging into my being and my soul was embracing the landscape. I realized that my place was here and I do not regret the decision I have made. For me, hiking and alpinism have always been a spiritual experience, a way of getting closer to heaven. On the summit of the Holy Mountain I felt that I was back home, to the place I had always belonged but had not understood yet."

His eyes got wet and mine too. After a long pause I wanted more, "And what do you mean by saying that alpinism is a spiritual experience?"

"Oh, you are touching on my favorite topic for discussion. Mountains do not move; mountains do not meet other mountains. We, as human beings, are the ones who meet others and learn from the mountains. When you go up a mountain, you are constantly being challenged like in your daily life. But, as in your life, the risks are minimized if you plan your path carefully. Behind every challenge is the continuous learning, body conditioning, determination towards a goal, and the use of previous experiences. Life is like hiking a mountain. At the same time that there is a strong desire to get to the summit, you must be prepared to go up, to know when to stop for rest, how to overcome challenges, and, if necessary, go down for a while before climbing up again, instead of forcing your way straight to the top.

"When you climb a mountain, the scenery changes and if you come to the same place where you had previously been, the way you look at that place may seem different than before. And that is also valid for our lives. When we climb all the mountains of our lives, frequently we find ourselves going in circles or returning to the same places. Nevertheless if we appreciate the journey and learn with the experiences and challenges we face along our way, returning to the same place will have a different meaning. Dealing with change, risk, success, and failure stretches our personal boundaries. After all, the risks of all journeys depend exclusively on the knowledge of what we are facing. The important thing to remember is that nobody else can choose or decide for you when to climb up a mountain; that decision is only yours. It is true that you must learn from the experiences of others, but the challenge is only yours, in your rhythm, in your own timing."

It was about time to get into the monastery before the doors closed. I thanked him for his teachings and went to bed. There are moments when you need no more reasoning, no more logic, no more talking. Just silence. Silence and surrender to the beauty of simple and touching moments like the ones I was experiencing.

The next day I left Great Lavra on my way to the skete of Saint-Anne, which belongs to the monastery although on the opposite side of the peninsula. It was going to be a long walk, more than five hours through the most rugged wilderness country in Athos.

Along the signposted trail I saw a hut with some icons on its outside. I got closer and saw a monk inside. He was painting. He was an iconographer!

As I paused to glance into his hut, he shuffled to its opening and called out politely, "Welcome. Please have a seat." .He motioned with his hands that I should join him in the primitive hut.

I sat on a chair facing a huge icon of the Virgin Mary with the child. "These icons look so rudimentary and lacking space," I thought.

"And what do you think of the *Axion Esti* icon?" he asked, pointing to the icon I was looking at.

"Is that the famous icon?" I asked, stirred up by listening to that multifaceted word again.

"Not really. This is a copy like most of the icons are," he shrugged.

"Being very candid," I said tentatively, "I was just thinking of how unnatural the icons look sometimes. They are very flat and lack emotion."

"I am listening to someone molded by Western culture," he reflected, not bothered by my criticism. "Let me explain to you what the true meaning of iconography is. After the Roman Empire was divided in two, the Empire of the West and the Empire of the East, in 330 AD Emperor Constantine founded a new capital on the ancient Greek city of Byzantium, occupying the region of Topkapy Palace in modern Istanbul, Turkey. He renamed it after himself as Constantinople. This move was partly motivated by religious purposes since Rome was deeply rooted in paganism.

"Constantinople, the new Rome, was destined to be the image of heaven on Earth and the emperor decreed that no pagan rites should ever be performed there. The emperor, surrounded by a rigorous structured governmental and ecclesiastical hierarchy, acted as God's representative on Earth while the patriarch of Constantinople was the head of the Church. Church and state sought jointly to unite heaven and Earth under the aegis of Christ. Religion entered into every aspect of Byzantine life including art."

He pointed to one of his icons. "Byzantine art developed into an entirely new style with spiritual purposes and was meant to be a 'visual theology.' The mosaics and icons achieved a restrained elegance, an emotional austerity and a 'cool' authoritative solemnity. Iconography developed as a way of having portable images that could be venerated at church and at home, carried in processions or when marching to war.

"Iconography is a liturgical art with the aim to comment on the divine world, to elevate the faithful. The beauty of liturgical painting is a beauty of the spirit, not of the flesh, striving to transmit the teachings of the Orthodox faith. When we look at the icon, it will invite us to pray. It is a window through which the observer silently communicates with the spiritual world."

He sat again by his work table and looked at me. "Those unfamiliar with icons may say that icons are just bi-dimensional and rudimentary. But icons deliberately play down the reality on Earth and the passions and elevate the soul. They are not meant to serve the passions but to soothe them. Human emotions, the self and personal ideas, have no place in iconography. In order to exhibit an inner change, the corporeal beings depicted manifest an outer change so that we can feel their sainthood, virtue, and immortality instead of passions and corruptibility.

"I have something here that will help you in perceiving the differences between Western and Byzantine art."

He went to a drawer and took out a big reproduction of the Virgin and the Child painted by Raphael, the famous painter from the Italian Renaissance. He placed it on the wall close to the *Axion Esti* icon and said,

"Comparing the Madonna and Child by Raphael and the Icon Theotokos Axion Esti, we find striking differences. Raphael's painting is more natural, more mundane. The Virgin and the child are part of a serene rural landscape with a church perched on a hill. The Virgin is almost smiling, almost praying, and entirely dedicated to her child, who embraces her, showing dependency to his mother and looking at us with abstracted sweetness. It seems like they came down to Earth although they maintain a higher position indicated by the position of their eyes looking down to the observer."

The hermit pointed to his work. "The icon, on the contrary, has a two-dimensional look in order to avoid realism and idolatry. The figures have exaggerated features. The Virgin's wide large almond-shaped eyes are intended to suggest her purity of heart, one who sees God. The forehead is large and high, expressing spiritual wisdom. The ears are large to listen to the words of God. The nose is drawn long and thin. The small mouth indicates the small amount of food needed to survive. Their postures are frontal and their faces have a stern expression. The halos, a symbol of holiness, reinforce the saintliness of the figures. The child holds in his hand a symbolic scroll since he is the guardian of the holy scripture. Specific hand gestures are applied to the Virgin and Jesus Christ. The child on her lap, as her Lord, can fend for himself and it is on us that she bends her inviting austere and maternal look as if saying, 'I am here for you.'

Icon Theotokos Axion Esti

Small Cowper Madonna from Raphael

"Folds in clothing are simplified and straight and are intended not so much to follow contours of the body, but to emphasize the incorporeal and spiritual nature of the subject. The use of gold backgrounds sets the figures apart from real time and space and symbolizes the divine light surrounding them. This unrealistic look of icons is intended to reveal a divine and spiritual world, different from ours."

He touched the area on his icon as he talked and I strained forward to follow his explanation. "Specific colors must be used. The Virgin Mary must always wear royal purple robes. Royal purple is the color of emperors and kings and hence she must always be painted in that specific color. Color is applied to make figures readable even at distance.

"Initials are seen in the upper corners of the icon to tell who the observers are viewing in the icon. Christ is shown with *IC* (Jesus) and *XC* (Christ) close to him."

"Father, it appears like style and the form are standardized," I commented. "Can't you use your creativity in producing icons?"

He shook his head decisively. "Iconographers like myself should, during their work, pray and fast. Individual interpretation should be kept to a minimum. My task is to pass on the tradition by replicating previous icons. Like a scribe copying the text of the Bible, I am only a vehicle through which the heavenly images are brought to the believers. While painting an icon, I am taken to heaven as the believer while venerating them."

"Father, would you mind if I stay silent around here, just observing the icons that you have painted? I will not disturb you," I promised, rising from my chair.

"Stay as long as you want and enjoy the spirituality of your inner silence in front of the icons. Silence is many times understood as a meaningless emptiness, a mere lack of words, thoughts, and feelings, an inner desert. In reality silence is a fundamental human dimension as in music, which is made of sounds and silence. Without pauses music would not exist. Without pauses our lives may result in a meaningless noise. Silence is the preliminary condition for any human communication, for emptying ourselves so that our vase can fill up again with our human experiences. Inner silence is the way of opening the gates of our senses and perception."

He resumed his painting and I stayed there for a long time, being transposed to another dimension by observing the icons. I studied details and tried to see each technique through his explanation so I might derive all their meaning.

I felt that during that short period in Athos my vase was overflowing with all those experiences and I decided to have a pause before moving on to Saint-Anne. Since every new step was filling my vase so quickly, I decided to go back to Lavra and request to stay one more night. At least I was acquainted with the monastery and this could give a needed pause before moving into the unknown again.

"Did you decide to stay longer with us?" the monk alpinist asked when I met him at the courtyard at Lavra.

I explained to him what had happened and about my decision of pausing and finding a safe harbor for a while. He listened carefully and answered, "Heraclito once said that 'you do not bathe twice in the same river. The second time neither you nor the river will be the same.' Your openness to what is new will create surprise, amazement, and bewilderment, which in turn will result in a new perspective of looking at the same things. Come with me."

He took me to one of the chapels. Behind it was a locked room. He opened it. On a table, at the end, an icon was illuminated by the feeble light of a candle. Suddenly I realized that I was being observed by hundreds of staring dark eyes. When my eyes adapted to the frail light, I saw skulls displayed in neat rows on the shelves all around, each one with a name. I was at the monastery's ossuary.

"This is scary. Why have you brought me here?" I asked him shuddering.

"Death according to Christian teachings is the passage from the corruptible world to eternal life. These skulls belonged to monks who dedicated most of their lives to the moment of their resurrection and to live their eternity in heaven side by side with our Lord. Some years ago the abbot assigned to me the task of assisting my brothers on this moment of passage. From those who nearly died but recovered I always heard that they had seen their entire lives in those instants. It was as if they were looking through a window from which they could see their choices, decisions, and accomplishments, what they could have done and did not, whom they had loved and whom they had hated."

He moved close to the rows of skulls as if to direct my gaze to them. "Life is made of cycles that create particular thresholds through which we are ushered at pivotal moments of our existence. Ending a cycle is always one of the hardest things we face because it brings a sentiment of attachment and loss as we leave the known limits of the old reality and venture into an unknown realm although these transitions will always stage a renewed vision of our true essence. Yet it is when we stare the inevitability of our own death in the face, the ultimate end, the ultimate transition towards another level of being or consciousness, a transition to immortality, that our whole perspective changes.

"However do not wait until the end of your life to find out your disappointments about what you might have done, might have been, might have become. Let me suggest that you start right now imagining that you are on your deathbed reviewing your life. What will cause you to look back with a sense of satisfaction? Or, putting it another way, how do you really want to measure the worth of your life?"

He waved his hand around the room and said, "Take another look around. Kings, emperors, tyrants, despots, rich people, poor people will all end like this. At the very end what makes you unforgettable is not what you have but what you did, how you contributed to the well-being of others. Despite inevitable death, man's enduring legacy is what makes him immortal in this world because he will live in the hearts and minds of those he left behind.

"Death is a central dynamism underlying life. Death exposures can invigorate individuals' pathways. There are plenty of examples of individuals who changed entirely their approach to life when they had near-death experiences. It is when one sees the horizon as an end that one first begins to see. And that's why I brought you here—so that you could be closer to the ultimate significance of life."

After a few minutes of silence he took me back to the courtyard again and continued, "Do not run from the mountains and deserts of your life. Do not take the ostrich approach of finding a hole to put your head into when you face a peril and pretend that the menace is gone. I admit that pauses and safe harbors are important, but do not turn away just because you think your vase is overflowing. Maybe what is overflowing is only waste. Probably the real content which is dense is sinking into your being. Do not run away from breathing the essence of this landscape and from hearing its wisdom."

"Father, once again many thanks for sharing all this knowledge with me. On the one hand I should not have returned but on the other hand I am happy I came back to Lavra so I could learn once more from your teachings."

"The wisdom and the teachings are not mine. They belong to this landscape," he replied humbly.

With his last words I also sensed that the Athos was gradually molding my personal pilgrimage's journal: believe and you will find it; *axion esti*; the echoes of the landscape. . . .

THE CAVE

Back on my path to Saint-Anne I passed again by the iconographer's hut and two hours later, after a densely forested ravine, I found a spot protected by an enormous walnut tree furnishing deep shade and with a nearby stream flowing down to the sea. The place was an invitation to rest, with the fantastic view of the Aegean in front of me and the calming music of the rolling waters.

"I am neither an ostrich nor an alpinist," I declared to myself. "I have my own rhythm and my own pauses to face the beauty that life can offer me. I will enjoy this landscape since I need to be at Saint-Anne only before the doors close."

I was lost in my relaxation when I turned to the right and saw a pair of penetrating eyes looking at me. He was a monk, I thought, although he looked much more like a beggar. He was so thin that his face was delineated by his skeleton even though hidden by his long white hair and beard. His appearance was fragile, but he demonstrated a lot of vitality. He gave me a large, sweet smile and said, "Don't be scared, my boy. I still belong to this world. What are you doing here?"

"I am on my way to Saint-Anne's skete and I was relaxing . . .?"

"No, no," and he smiled again. "I asked you what are you doing in Athos?"

"I came here as a result of a desire that bred for years inside me. And so far this has been a touching experience."

"Good, good. Tell me what do you do for a living."

"My background is engineering."

"Ula, ula, a very rational human being. But please I do not mean to depreciate you because you are an engineer. Years ago I was a famous architect in Greece, a very logical and rational person, working like mad with the only objective of becoming rich and enjoying life. But, if you work desperately to become rich, you do not have time to enjoy life, right? And at a certain point I decided to stop working and only enjoy all the pleasures of life. Then I realized that there was something missing inside me. And this missing feeling I was able to fulfill only when I came to Athos."

"But don't you miss the secular world?" I asked, trying not to stare at his dirt-blackened feet.

"Of course I missed it in the beginning. Before I arrived here, I was living each day of my life as if it would be the last. I was very anxious on a desperate search for the indulgence of all my senses. And the more I sustained that style, the more empty I felt inside until I realized that my fashion of life was only smoke in the air. What I learned later on was exactly the opposite, or how to free myself from the passions and attachments of daily life. This training or struggle, so to speak, is called asceticism and is part of monastic life. Asceticism leads to a state in which we are no longer under the dominion of such impulses, making us capable of feeling and sharing genuine love. Fasts, minimum amount of sleep, celibacy, and an austere lifestyle, which are part of asceticism, are not to be taken as a rejection of the body but as the acquisition of dominion over it, enabling us to say no without which we can never say yes. Despite its great importance this training is a means, not an end. Once attachments to the senses and passions are transcended, attachments to the intellect and imagination remain. Mental or inner practices need to be used to release those attachments."

"I have to admit that this sounds confusing to me," I said, shaking my head.

"Let me give you an example, my boy. One who is addicted to wine does not enjoy wine. It is only when one can say no to wine that one can truly enjoy it. In the end asceticism is the ultimate hedonism. Without asceticism pleasures are lost in a sea of necessity and we become prisoners to the passions that rule our lives. Bound by our desires we are kept in a dreamland where we perceive our confinement as freedom and our chains as wings. But all this illusion turns into a feeling of anxiety and of something missing inside you that can only be overcome when you exercise the power of controlling your body."

I stared off into the distance for a moment and then replied, "That is indeed an interesting argument. However I do not know if this is for me."

"It all depends on how you feel and what your needs are. If this was for everybody, Athos would be full of skyscrapers and I would be planning apartment complexes around here!" The hermit laughed.

"That's very true," I answered. "And how about withdrawal from society? Don't you miss the interaction with other people?"

"Am I not interacting with you at this moment? You are the society's representative at this point."

"I am sorry, I did not mean . . . ," I responded quickly.

"Please, do not be sorry. I was only joking. As you can see, depending on each one, withdrawal can have some flexibility, even for a hermit like me."

"But why flee the comforts of life and adopt such a harsh life?" I pressed.

"Withdrawal is the other component of the puzzle because in fleeing we abandon the many distractions surrounding us in the secular world. Worldly renunciation is a tool to compensate for personal weakness because it is not through virtue that we live in solitude but through weakness.

"The call to retreat is also mystical and has a biblical basis. The time that Jesus spent in the wilderness, with all its physical deprivation and supernatural struggle, was claimed as a model by the early Christians, who followed his example and went into the desert. There they had their battle against hunger and thirst, against the desire for sleep, against extreme heat and cold, against demons and apparitions, against loneliness, and against the lusts and imaginations of the mind. These early Christians, many of whom became saints, are known as the Desert Fathers. And this area from Lavra to Saint-Anne is called the desert of Athos because this is the preferred region for hermits like myself. But who has lived and not at some instant heard, however faintly, this call? In the busiest moments, in the most absorbed, who has not felt this inexplicable desire for solitude, for a place of silence and peace in which to make sense of one's own life and the world's stage?"

He looked at me intensely. "This was certainly my real motivation in coming to Athos," I admitted. "The days and nights I have stayed here have sparked a transformation inside me. Hearing all that you are saying now, I am wondering what an experience it could be to stay in a hut for just one day."

"Do you really want to experience what a hermit life means?"

"Are you serious?" I asked.

"Of course I am. We even have a cave for guests. Well, I am just kidding, but in reality there is a cave from a monk who died a few years ago and has not been occupied since then. Do you want to take a look?"

"I would love to!"

The hermit took me along a precipitous track cut on the vertical cliff to a cave not far from where we had been. My heart was beating at fast pace when I entered the hut. The place seemed like it had been carved by generations of hermits along the centuries. The cave had an entrance leading to an area like a living room. The hermit sat on an armchair sculpted from the rock and let me explore the space for a while. I saw some stairs disappearing into the rock and I climbed them to see where they were leading. It was an area with space for someone to lay down and rest, with sort of a rock pillow on one end. The hermit called from the living room, "The alignment of the bed and the pillow have a purpose." He ascended the stairs to stand beside me. "You lay down on an east-west axis with your eyes facing east, facing Jerusalem, from where the light comes. That's actually the way the early Christians were buried, with their heads facing east, awaiting their resurrection in the hands of the Lord. Every night you sleep in here will be like when you will await your renaissance for the other life."

"Please, Father, do not frighten me," I shuddered, backing up towards the entrance of the room.

"No, my boy, I am not frightening you. I am just helping you enhance your experience. But if you do not feel like staying here, please, I am not forcing you."

"No, no, that's something I want to experience," I responded quickly.

"If so, there are a few things I must tell you. Do not think this will be an easy stay. It will not. After all you are not in a cave as part of an adventure tour but as a way of knowing who you really are, what your true essence is, and how you can find inner peace no matter how hectic your life can be. It is a step towards something bigger than you. Finding yourself can be tough, but do not panic. All these days you have been introduced, in a certain way, to control your body, to reduce your food intake, and to detach yourself from the secular world through pilgrimage and prayer. Now it is time for a bigger and more difficult leap, which is the transcendence over the intellect and imagination. This is not a one-day struggle, but all journeys must begin with a first step, right?"

"And what's my first step?" I asked hesitantly.

"You must learn to be still, preferably in a sitting or kneeling position. Pay attention to your breath and try to calm it down, inhaling and exhaling slowly. Stillness is the preparatory step to prayer. It's your own effort to be still that gives rise to prayer. The resulting fruits and benefits are an internal and external change, for the better, of yourself.

"When you have calmed down, pray mentally, '*Kyrie eleison (Lord Jesus Christ, have mercy on me),*' following the rhythm of your breath. Now take my prayer rope; you will need it. Sit down close to me and let's try it." The prayer rope consisted of 100 knots so the user could keep track of the number of his prayers.

I sat on the floor, closed my eyes, and listened to the hermit. "Close your eyes. Pay attention to your breath. Breathe in, breathe out slowly. Think of your breath as the link between your heart and your mind. With your breath and your prayer rope you will calm down your mind and open up your heart. With the flow of your breath pray mentally, '*Kyrie eleison, kyrie eleison, kyrie eleison.*' Use the prayer rope to facilitate the repetition and keep attention on your breath. Do not let your mind use you. Remember, you must be in control. Breathe out and let your thoughts go away, breathe in and expand your heart, always with the vibrations of '*kyrie eleison, kyrie eleison, kyrie eleison.*'"

A long pause followed. I was trying to bond to my prayer, but temptations were all around, in my body starting to itch, in my wandering thoughts. "What is he doing now?" I thought. I opened my eyes slowly just to find that he was staring at me. And he said, "This is normal. I told you that it is not easy to give power and momentum to this capability of our souls. Normally our bodies, thoughts, and ideas are stronger. That's why I gave you a prayer rope, as a way to have an external reference, to calm down your senses which are most of the time concerned with the externals. Sit facing the icon and let's try again.

"Face the icon and pray, *'Kyrie eleison, kyrie eleison, kyrie eleison.'* Use your prayer rope and repeat it 100 times. When you feel ready to go into yourself, close your eyes. And after you have completed 100 times, relax, walk around, and do 100 more until you reach a thousand. *Kyrie eleison, kyrie eleison, kyrie eleison.*"

When I opened my eyes, I noticed that the hermit had disappeared, leaving myself with myself in the middle of nowhere, with a prayer rope in my hand. I started exploring my hut carved into the Holy Mountain. I sat on the armchair. The view was magnificent. The amazing blue in front of me disclosing a combination of Earth, sea, sky, and heavens was capable of creating a feeling of joyfulness and at the same time intimidation in the face of the horizons.

After a while I stood up and went to the cave's "door." I looked to the right and to the left and saw no neighbors. I noticed, more to the left, a pulley. I took a closer look down and I could only see the pulley's rope disappearing over the vertical cliff going straight into the sea. I pulled the rope. It was long and at its end was an empty bucket. Then I realized that this was the preferred method used by the most strict hermits for hoisting up supplies offered from passing boats. Since they are mainly occupied with prayer, they eat just enough to stay alive and they drink rain water which they collect and store.

"This must be their daily workout. Pull up the pulley and discover what the Divine Providence is offering them," I thought. I decided to put the bucket back down again, expecting to see what I would get during my stay, and went back to my armchair.

After a while and the initial excitement, each fleeting instant began to resemble the face of eternity. I had to find a way of not being bored and not considering the cave a prison but a temple of self-renewal and discovery. But it was not easy and I imagined all those hermits along the centuries, some living for years in a place like the one I was in. It is either a path to sainthood or to madness from an excess of hardship and solitude. "I will not go nuts in one day," I reassured myself. But the more I moved around or thought about my daily habits, the more tense I got.

Suddenly I remembered the words of the hermit: "Do not let your mind control you, keep still, breathe, and pray mentally, '*Kyrie eleision.*'. I had 900 times more to finish the prayers of the day. I continued by intercalating them with conscious awareness of how my mind was manipulating me, some mobility around my hut, and relaxation on the armchair. That armchair had a position from where one had a broad view framed by the cave's entrance. It was like a window into infinity. I sat there for a long time watching the sunset, the changing colors of the sky, the first stars announcing the coming night, and then the sky covered by stars everywhere.

What a sky! I had not seen one like that for a long time. It was beautiful but at the same time intimidating. The size of the universe strains our imagination. Looking out into space is like looking back in time, igniting a kind of intellectual hunger, a need to know who we are and how we got here. It is a permanent search for a cosmic perspective for humanity. In front of that universe I felt naked under my dark inner sky. I began to recollect the revelation of my possibilities within the caverns of my own being.

I was focusing on my inner ear and at the same time observing that immeasurable universe. A sense of smallness, impotence, fragility, and fear beyond the unknown took over me and I cried for a long time. Those tears washed me internally. I picked up the prayer rope, calmed my breath down, and prayed, "*Kyrie eleison, kyrie eleison, kyrie eleison.*" I had 400 more prayers to go.

Gradually that never-ending feeling of insignificance was transforming into a perception of the great magnitude of life itself, into a sentiment of being larger than my physical body. I sensed that I was expanding. The universe was in me and I was in the universe, in communion with the universe. And I kept praying until I repeated, *"Kyrie eleison"* 1,000 times.

When I finished, I opened my eyes. I was in front of that window to infinity and I was experiencing that infinitude inside me. That spark of boundlessness was pushing me far beyond my footprints. The emotion was intense and I decided to go to the "resurrection chamber" to allow time to absorb all that. "Pauses, how needed they always are, " I thought. I laid down on my bed with flourishing emotions of empowerment and fulfillment. It was not a logical comprehension but something that gradually impregnated my whole body and that I will never forget.

Suddenly I was holding a mirror in front of two diverging roads and trying to decide which road to take. I was surrounded by three beautiful ladies, one holding a spool, the second pulling thread, and the third one snipping it. When I looked at myself in the mirror, I was two headed with two opposing heads.

"What a dream," I shuddered, sitting up from my rock bed. "What is the meaning of all that?" It seems like the two-headed eagle on the Byzantine flag was not enough and I was awarded with two opposing heads during my dream. I wandered to the living room. Through my window to infinity the sun was beginning to rise. No better moment to start my prayers than in front of all that beauty that nature was presenting me.

When I finished, my mind was on the bucket. I hurried to the pulley, pulled the rope up, and found three peaches. I did not know who had offered them, but I savored each of the peaches slowly and with much pleasure. After all I had not recovered from the "trauma" of letting the peaches at the table of Simonopetra go uneaten. "What a coincidence. But it is too much coincidence to be only a coincidence," I thought. I enjoyed the peaches so much that I began questioning if that was that the beginning of my experience with true hedonism.

"Is the real essence of life to share and receive with no intent except one of loving and being capable of appreciating the simple things of life?" I asked myself.

When the hermit reappeared later that morning, I was excited and full of enthusiasm. He smiled, "Calm down, calm down. Remember, be still, breathe, and pray."

We left the cave and walked back to the path to Saint-Anne.

"Father, I do not know where to start," I blurted out. "Probably with the bizarre dream I had last night."

I glanced often at his face while I told him the details of my dream. When I finished, he commented. "It was a very symbolic dream. You were in front of the crossroads of your life. What did the crossroads, the forking of the ways, really mean?" He walked on a way in silence as if carefully forming his answer.

He stopped along the path, picked up a stick, and circumspectly designed a huge Greek letter gamma (γ) on the soil. He commented, "Pythagoras was born in 582 BC on the Greek island of Samos in the Aegean Sea. He is most commonly remembered for his famous theorem although he was primarily a mystic and philosopher. His school was an institution of learning and a sanctuary for the cultivation of the spirit. Members took vows of loyalty and adhered to strict rules. He was one of the first feminists and equally admitted women, giving them the same basic education: philosophy, mathematics, music, and arts. Pythagoras has had a profound impact on philosophy, religion, and science, and he deeply influenced the number symbolism found in the teachings and liturgies of the Church.

"One of his famous sayings is 'Above all, have respect for yourself.'"

The hermit pointed to the letter he had drawn. "Pythagoras forged this two-horned symbol as the representation of life and the many crucial decisions we are always facing. However his genius was not aware that he was also creating a letter of the Greek alphabet.

"Gamma reaches to heaven with its right-hand horn while the left one seems to curve down towards Earth. Life is made of choices, goals, obstacles, and ways of overcoming the difficulties of a journey. The left horn represents the pleasant and easy way with its descending path. It is worn smooth by the tracks of many, but the destination is miserable and bitter. For those who enter the path to the right, the ascending path, the efforts are huge, it bears the footprints of only very few, but the rewards are the highest. The course of human life resembles the letter γ because every human, at the thresholds where the roads divide, is in doubt, hesitates, and does not know to which side to turn: to the difficult one leading up to higher and better achievements or to the one sloping down, a lot easier but preventing him from growing and gaining knowledge along the way. The crossroads which confront us are places of major significance, but this is what life is all about with its quests and trials sculpting our humanity."

Beside his symbol he drew an 8. "Gamma is also related to the number 8, which has so much meaning among the three major religions, having the ancient testament as their basis: for the Hebrews the 8 meant 'man'; for the Muslims, 'the infinite;' and for the Christians, 'resurrection.' Gamma unites all this symbolism since it resembles a man with open arms to the infinite with faith in his resurrection.

"The three ladies surrounding you represent the past, the present, and the future. The choices you made and the experiences you had in the past are responsible for what you are today, but if you do not like what you see looking at yourself in the mirror, you can always decide how your future can be. The lady holding the spool represents the present, what you have and how you can act to transform it. The lady holding the thread represents the past, the thread that came from the labyrinth through which you overcame the many difficulties of life. The third lady is snipping the continuation of the thread. She is the future, representing the choices yet to come."

He watched me while I studied his two symbols and let his words take root in me. "This is life, my boy. But the best thing in your dream was your two heads."

"My two heads?" I asked. "So probably this has some symbology analogous with the two-headed eagles on the Byzantine flag?"

He shook his head. "Not exactly. Janus was a Roman god with a double-faced head, each looking in opposite directions: what is behind and what lies ahead. He was the guardian of gates and portals, beginnings and endings, of all that is double-edged in life, and therefore was worshipped at all events related to change and transitions. Janus was characterized in such a distinct fashion due to the notion that doors and gates look in two directions and his name was the obvious choice for the name of the first month of the year, January, representative of contemplation on the happenings of an old year while looking forward to the new.

"Like Janus your two heads are the symbol of your inward journey, the capability that you are developing of looking outwards and inwards, looking backwards and ahead, to the past and the future, and of making the right choices.

"Since you are beginning your inward journey, you must use some tools. Your prayer rope is represented by the mirror, which symbolizes a tool to look inwards. And the Ariadne's thread of all this is what you are beginning to practice, the art of discipline, persistence, stillness, concentration, and silence. Associate all this with prayer and gradually you will unveil your true essence, the comprehension that you are made from the same nature as God. When asked by the Pharisees when the kingdom of God was coming, Jesus answered that 'it is not coming with signs to be observed. The kingdom of God is within you.'"

Again he paused while I pondered his words. "This stillness or inward silence is known in Greek as *hesychia*. This is the key. The repentance, spiritual discipline, and contemplative prayer through which the monk strives to see the light of God were articulated by the 14th-century Saint Gregory Palamas, who was a monk on Athos. His hesychastic philosophy included treatises on why the prophet is better equipped than the philosopher to understand God.

"Always pray to disengage from your thoughts. Focus your attention on how they emerge and flow, and do not be bound by them. With time and practice, detachment is facilitated. Emptying your mind of its thinking routines is a process we can only initiate like taking the stopper out of a bathtub. You don't have to push the water out of the tub; you simply allow it to run out."

"When you pray, you are doing something similar, allowing your train of thoughts to flow out of you. What you have learned is part of a long tradition and wisdom from the Desert Fathers called Prayer of the Heart. There is no better treasure and this is your key to a higher spirituality."

I kneeled down, held his two hands, and whispered, "Father, I do not know how to thank you for the teachings and the experience you shared with me."

"Stand up, my boy," he frowned. "I did nothing more than show you the path. The merit will be only yours in following it."

I handed the prayer rope back to him and the hermit insisted, "No, no, take it with you. You will need it for a long time. As I have mentioned, the path is simple, but it is not easy. Follow the path with perseverance and moderation, trying to prevent the temptations, distracting cares, and overindulgences you will find along the way. And always try to open your heart and from its depths offer your prayers to God. Go, my boy, go and find the shining jewel inside you."

The hermit embraced me and said, "In love we are speechless; in awe words fail us."

And he left without saying more words. Under that same tree where I had met the hermit the day before, I stayed still and silent for a long time.

9

THE JOURNEY HOME

Once more I was on the way to Saint-Anne. Only then I realized that I had not learned the hermit's name. And for him I was only "my boy." I was walking on the same holy mountain as the day before, but my perspective had totally changed.

The path had stunning scenery from the peninsula's southwestern coast and the buildings of Saint-Anne on its ravine. I walked and reflected about what all those hermits were searching for. After all, their search is not different from ours although they may accentuate certain notes more than we do. Most of them will succeed, some will fail, but all of them deserve our admiration and respect.

A few hours later I was at Saint-Anne, from where I took the ferry to Ouranopolis via Daphne. On the deck pilgrims were returning home or moving between the monasteries. At the prow I noticed quite a character. He had long, curled black hair and was dressed all in white. He was standing erect and holding an engraved ivory walking stick. He had a very aristocratic appearance and a contained elegance. He was in a contemplative mode, still like a statue. Moved by curiosity, I went to the prow.

When I got closer to him, he asked, "What are you doing in Athos, foreigner?"

"And how do you know I am a foreigner?" I asked him, unnerved.

"Because you don't smell like a Greek. I am blind by birth and for this reason I developed my other senses and my olfaction in particular. Probably by the same way that you separate and recognize colors, I am capable of recognizing the spectrum of odors.

"The soul of the land where you live is imprinted on you, giving different nuances of aromas for the people from diverse territories. That is how I can recognize if you are Greek or not. We are all like the great wines, always liberating specific bouquets. Like wines some people are more sweet, others more dry. Some more complex, some more simple in their structure. Some more astringent, others more smooth. Each one with his particular character. Unfortunately some individuals do not realize the superior wine they are made of and they let themselves turn into vinegar."

He turned towards me and continued, "And that is how I compensate my blindness, by getting into others' souls and recognizing their individual fragrance. You, for example, are carrying notes of an elaborate person but not from Greece."

"You are right; I am not Greek," I said. "And I did not know that I could be compared to a wine. That is quite interesting."

"And let me tell you," he added, grinning, "you are a wine of superb quality!"

We laughed and for a while I described to him the different "bottles" sitting around the boat and he figured out if the appearance of their container was compatible with the wine inside. After a while he commented, "Although I cannot see any of the 'bottles' around, I can guarantee that after a stay in Athos they all have new wine in their old pots. If they will let this wine age correctly is another problem."

"Tell me, how did you get this fixed idea on wines?" I asked.

"Wine is an experience open to invention and reinvention, a permanent invitation to life. This invitation is not answered with excesses but on capturing the pleasure of tasting it. It is like in life where we must learn to harvest its many flavors, capturing the small everyday pleasures while seeking to exorcise the causes of dissatisfaction. This continuous harvest should be jealously overseen and protected like the best vintage in a cellar.

"The lengthy process of growing in knowledge and appreciation of wine is a journey without real destination since you will never reach an end because there are always many roads to choose. It takes a poet within to enjoy and make a great wine.

He twirled his walking stick as he paused. Then he continued, "This is how I make my living. I help wineries produce top-quality premium wines. In Greece I am trying hard to convince my clients to stop using exogenous varietals and preserve the indigenous ones such as the Nemea Aghiorghitiko. It produces a full-bodied wine with spectacular bouquets of black currant and damson. Excavations in Nemea, where Heracles did the first of his 12 labors, found 5,000-year-old seeds with the same chemical composition as the present grapes. Drinking an Aghiorghitiko is to celebrate with god Dyonisus the ecstasy produced by this elixir from heaven. It was exported to the Greek nation scattered around the Mediterranean, and later on to the Roman Empire, through the city of Corinthos, one of the largest, most powerful and wealthiest cities of ancient Greece. In 51 AD St. Paul, the apostle, stayed there for 18 months to preach the Christian faith. Wine and spirituality, always together.

"Wine has always been an integral part of life on Mount Athos. Their 850-year-old vineyards are tended by monks. During the harvest there are no songs nor dances but only prayers thanking the Creator for the crop and the discreet sound of the scissors. Today we witness in many monasteries a revival of this rich heritage of viticulture and wine production which culminated in 1981 with the recognition of the Mount Athos local wine, the first Greek local wine to be recognized by the European Economic Community.

"With my assistance they are beginning to produce excellent wines like Mount Athos from the Agios Pandeleimon's Monastery, a medal winner and a deliciously complex red.

He turned his face again in my direction. "And how about you? Tell me about your experiences in Athos., Tell me about the new wine you have within."

When I finished telling him about all the experiences I had during the past few days, he asked, "And where are you going now?"

"I hope to be back home in two days."

"Foreigner, don't rush yourself. Good wines become even better when they age appropriately. Make long your way home."

"What do you mean by this?" I asked, puzzled.

He shook his walking stick in my direction for emphasis. "When you set out on your journey home, pray that the road is long, full of adventure, full of knowledge. But do not hurry the voyage at all. It is better to let it last for many years. Finally when you get there, wise as you have become, you must already have understood what home means.

"This is a poem from a renowned Greek poet named Cavafis. His poem, 'Ithaca,' is related to the *Odyssey*. Have you read the *Odyssey*?"

"Not yet," I answered sheepishly.

"You should. The *Odyssey* is an epic poem. It was composed 3,000 years ago to be recited to the accompaniment of a lyre to a listening audience. Homer began by invoking the muses, the nine daughters of Zeus, the inspiring spirits of all the arts and sciences. In a noble and pungent mode he said, 'Sing in me, Muses, and through me tell the story of Odysseus, that man who traveled all the world and is skilled in all ways of contending.'

Homer's epic poems educated Greece and provided the values by which life should be lived. Since then this epic has ignited the Western imagination."

"Why is that?" I asked him.

"The *Odyssey* from Homer tells how Odysseus returned from Troy to his home in Ithaca. Even for the astute Odysseus, who had devised the Trojan horse to win the legendary battle of Troy, it was not an easy journey. The poem is about the setbacks he faced along his way that caused a short trip to become a 10-year journey of trials around the Mediterranean Sea. On a deeper level this is a voyage of personal transformation. Odysseus goes through hell on his way home, as most of us do.

"Along his journey Odysseus lost much of the pride with which he began. The homeward journey was marked by a process of constant attrition. He started with 12 ships and a crew of soldiers. At the end he was alone, naked and holding onto a log to survive. Symbolically he was stripped from the various supports on which he had relied during his journey, a loss that allowed him to know in a totally new sense who he really was. Odysseus learned a courage that was different from the cunning and aggressiveness of the battlefield—a courage to discover his inner kingdom, his way home."

"That is not very different from what we are looking for in Athos," I commented.

I led him to a deck chair and sat in one beside him. "That is very correct," he replied. "During the Odysseys of our lives Athos is a place that must be always included in our itinerary. However no matter the trials and experiences you may have had during the days you were in Athos, that is not enough. The longer the way home, the better because we must expose ourselves to the unexpected, always learning something new but always mindful of our goal, our true destination.

"We must follow the advice of Homer's poems to behold the customs and cities of many lands and peoples, to contemplate with curiosity forests, mountains, seas, lakes, springs, and rivers. It is not sufficient to visit places and enjoy them; we must learn from them with a fusion of curiosity, desire for the new, and unwillingness to settle down. This journey, needless to say, is life.

"Nikos Kazantzakis, who became famous because of his book, *Zorba The Greek*, created a sequel to Homer's epic poem, beginning where Homer left off. After his arrival in Ithaca Odysseus becomes thoroughly bored and sails again on a journey to explore the world. Kazantzakis explains the meaning of his sequel to Homer's epic poem as 'I am a mariner of Odysseus with heart afire but with mind ruthlessly clear; not, however, of that Odysseus who returned to Ithaca and stayed there but the other Odysseus who returned, killed his enemies and stifled in his native land, put out to sea once more.'

"And have you questioned yourself why only men are allowed in Athos?" he asked me.

"Certainly. To avoid the temptations of the opposite sex," I responded with assurance.

"You are only surfacing the real issue, my dear. To get the real answer let's get back to the *Odyssey*. During Odysseus's journey it is not by chance that help and insights came from women.

"After 10 years at the blood-bathed plains of Troy the heroic male became indifferent to killing, destruction, raping, and suffering. After years of war, fighting for his life and for the heroic ideal, he was acutely traumatized. Now he is coming home yearning for relationship, non-aggression, tenderness, a need to reconnect with his feelings and emotions, the feminine within him. It is to the wisdom of the opposite sex that he must turn to find his way home, toward his feminine counterpart. It is not a coincidence that Odysseus spends seven years of his return in a cave on the luxuriant island of Ogygia with the beautiful and seductive Calypso."

"Don't tell me that these seven years in the cave are related to the symbolic meaning of the number seven as steps to virtue and wisdom and more specifically about his new development in a uterus represented by a cave," I blurted out.

"Bravo." He tapped his walking stick on the deck in approval. "I can see that you have been doing your homework. Calypsos's name means 'cover' and in reality Odysseus's long stay is nothing less than a rebirth in the cave, the womb, where he gradually 'covers' all that he has known of life. And like most of us Odysseus is slow to unlearn that the time for playing the hero, with his armor on, has passed."

"But what does this have to do with no women in Athos?" I asked.

"Calm down, do not be so anxious. I am getting there.

"The one and only purpose of the great journey of life is the integration of our masculine and feminine counterparts. This is the inner kingdom. For some the road is easier, for others more difficult. For some it is longer, and for others shorter. But for all of us the goal is the same: to return home. We progress along different paths, but with similar footsteps, and by different roads we all seek the same goal. And in Athos it is not different. Why is Athos called the garden of the Virgin Mary? Why is the most venerated icon in Athos the *Axion Esti*? Why is the Holy Mountain the Virgin's mountain? To all these questions the answer is the same. To maintain the monks focused on their ultimate goal, the encounter with the divine, the union of their masculine and feminine, the eclipse of their duality on their way to the portal of the unity.

"After being constantly confronted by impassable places and endless monsters, after having unlearned the whole style of mastering the world, after resisting the temptations to abandon the journey and docking forever at some gorgeous place, harmed and tired, covered by mud and dust, we finally arrive home just to find that there is no welcoming committee. Home is just the place where we have always belonged. And in Athos there is no place for the external feminine because the signposts of the Virgin Mary, serving as a lighthouse pointing to the monks'

83

internal feminine, and ultimately to their unity threshold, are more than enough."

I was thrilled, surprised, and aroused. That explanation overwhelmed me. Unfortunately the ferry was docking at Daphne. A car was waiting for the blind man.

"Where are you going?" I asked.

"To the monastery of Vatopedi. That's where Britain's Prince Charles stays during his frequent stays. There he has his own room and office."

"But why is he coming to Athos?" I asked.

"You haven't even read the *Odyssey* yet, so why rush to know why Prince Charles is coming frequently to Athos ? Keep your own path, my dear."

I grabbed his arm to detain him. He stiffened. "Can't you tell me anything more? This was one of my fervent questions when I came to Athos."

He stopped and turned towards me. "Just because you are wine of superb quality. But first of all let me tell you that you do not have the slightest idea of what you are stirring up asking this question. To solve the puzzle you need to look at his coat of arms. On its right is a representation of a unicorn. In heraldry the unicorn represents not only Scotland, but interestingly enough it also represents purity, chastity, and virginity and in Western Christian symbolism the unicorn was used to represent the Virgin Mary until forbidden by the Roman Catholic Council of Trent in the 14th century because of lack of real proof of its existence. On its left there is a composite animal with the head of a lion, body of a leopard, and feet of a bear. These are the animal symbols for France, the leopard; Germany, the bear; and England, the lion. These nations represented the western arm of the Holy Roman Empire.

"Prince Charles Philip Arthur George, the future King George VII, has plenty of titles reflecting his wealth, supremacy, and power. He is related to all of the royal houses of Europe and his lineage goes back to Charlemagne and to the ancient kingdoms of Persia, Babylon, and Jerusalem. Follow the 7, my dear, there is always something behind it.

Coat of Arms of Prince Charles

"From his office at Vatopedi, in the garden of the Virgin Mary, His Royal Highness wants to look at his roots and learn from two of the most influential teachers of his ancestors: Socrates, who laid the foundations of Western Civilization's intellectual framework, and Jesus, the father of Christianity. Neither of them wrote a book. Socrates was immortalized by the writings of Plato and Jesus by the apostles. Both sought to reroute individuals from wandering aimlessly through life to following their true paths. Like the gods in the *Odyssey*, they wanted to guide their students or disciples to find their way home.

"His Highness is also after his true path and, why not say, he also wants to fulfill his duties of governance by getting closer to one of the greatest spiritual traditions as a way of extending his power and control. After all, like in the Byzantine Empire, the secular and the spiritual power continue to be together in present Greece."

"Aren't the two powers separated in Greece?" I asked.

"Not yet, my dear. Just as an example, the Orthodox priests in Greece are considered as public servants and are paid by the Greek state. Byzantium is still alive in Greece. The prince is taking advantage of his stays in Mount Athos to learn useful lessons from the past. Anyway we will need to wait until his coronation to see how much he became molded by the history, the tradition, and the Greek philosophers."

The blind man continued on his way to Vatopedi on the other side of the peninsula. And I stayed for a long time at the café in Dafni, waiting for the arrival of the *Axion Esti* ferry to Ouranopolis. My mind was moving fast and trying to make sense of all I had heard and the connectedness of all I had lived. Coincidence? Probably not.

I was beginning to unearth a symbolic world of the past lost in the shadows of the rational thinking of our present society. It is not that the ancients, who believed in unicorns, were less clever than we are. Their intelligence was turned in a different direction. To find the unicorn, as the ancients did, we have to unlearn what we have learned, we must go back to an earlier way of looking at the world. This is also a way of understanding who we are today. Like intellectual archeologists we must brush away the dust from our buried past as a step toward creating the future we want.

Pilgrimage is a bridge that can take us from where we presently are to somewhere else with a higher meaning and content. In ancient Rome when a bridge was constructed, a sacrifice was offered to the divinity protecting the place. The ritual was celebrated by the Pontifex Maximus, a title assumed later on by the Caesars and since the fifth century by the Pope as the "bridge constructor" between this world and the divine. With my pilgrimage to Athos I could now realize that this was my time to seize that title and assume my Pontifex Maximus condition between myself and my inner kingdom, my real home. The world inside was yearning for the stimulation that would open up its doors.

I finally crossed through customs and boarded the *Axion Esti*. I felt like I had wings to take me to a higher meaning in my life. My body and soul had absorbed not only part of the eternal peace and spirituality that have been preserved by tradition and the ideals of the monastic way of life but a lot more from the wisdom of those whom I met along the way.

The *Axion Esti* ferry docked at Ouranopolis and I slowly walked back again into the 21st century to take the bus back to Athens.

I thought about the beginning of my journey when I was facing the two gates of Athens leading to Eleusis and Plato's Academy. I did not know then that I would find a Christian world so rooted in Plato's legacy and on the appropriation of pagan rituals. The two gates date back 2,500 years and yet are so present with the teachings they convey.

I looked at the tavern where I went the first night and remembered the old lady who said that Athos would not be a visit but a journey deep into my soul. "She was right," I thought. I could also hear the crickets persisting with their tuning symphony. Everything seemed to be exactly the same as when I left except that, with the eyes I had in the beginning, I would say that my journey was coming to an end. Now I can only say that this end is the dawn of a new beginning.

GLOSSARY

anchorite – Derived from the *anakhoretes* meaning "one who withdraws from the world for religious reasons." It is understood as a synonym to *hermit, ascetic*, and *monk*.

ascetics – The suppression of the body for spiritual ends. The Pauline references to the "flesh" were taken as meaning the body rather than our sinful nature. The injunction to "mortify the flesh" was understood as literal. In such a framework of understanding, there was much in the New Testament that seemed to be a call to asceticism (e.g., Romans 8:13 or 1 John 2:15). *Ascetic* is derived from the Greek word *asketikos*, "one who is rigorously self-disciplined," and from *askein*, "one who exercises or trains." It refers to a solitary self-disciplined living exercising to imitate Christ. It is understood as a synonym to *hermit, anchorite*, and *monk*.

Axion Esti – The name of a hymn sung at the Divine Liturgy. It is also the name of the most celebrated icon on the Holy Mountain, which is preserved in the sanctuary of the church of Protaton in Charies.

basilica – Roman public building. Its design was applied to Christian churches in early Christianity. A basilican church had its entrance on the west and the altar on the east.

Byzantine – Byzantium was the Greek colony founded in 668 BC at the entrance of the Bosphorus, where Constantine established the new capital of the Roman Empire in 330 AD and renamed it Constantinople. It gave its name to the empire as a whole and also to the distinctive art present in icons. After the Ottoman conquest of Constantinople in 1453 it was renamed Istanbul although the Greeks still call it by the old name.

calendar – The term originates from the Roman word *calare,* which meant "to announce solemnly the first day of each month," referred to as *kalends.*

Catholic – The term means "universal" and designated the Western Latin-speaking Church that accepted the primacy of the Pope at Rome.

Constantine I – "The Great" (emperor, 306-337). He reunited the Roman Empire in 324. He was the first Christian emperor. He summoned the First Ecumenical Council (325) and built Constantinople (330), presently named Istanbul in Turkey.

dokimos – A Greek word that means "the one who tries." It is the term given for those who are on a probation period to become monks. A novice.

Ecumenical Councils – The first seven councils were summoned with representatives of the entire Christian world and articulated and defined the fundamental doctrines: the First Ecumenical Council (325) in Nicaea and the Second (381) in Constantinople ruled in favor of the Trinity. The Third (431) in Ephesus upheld Mary as the Mother of God. The Fourth (451) in Chalcedon ruled in favor of the two natures of Christ. The Fifth (553) in Constantinople condemned the Nestorian writings. The Sixth (681) in Constantinople condemned the Monophysite and Monothelete doctrines. The Seventh (787) in Nicaea restored the veneration of icons.

ekklesia – In ancient Greece and Rome this was the assembly of all adult male citizens, those entitled to participate in political life. This word came into Christianity to denote the church or the place where the faithful assembled to worship God.

enthusiasm – Comes from the Greek word *enthousiasmos,* meaning "to have the God inside you, to be possessed by the God."

hermit – Since the third century AD Christians started adopting ascetic forms of self-discipline, seeking religious insight through solitude and ecstatic experience. First they inhabited the desert lands of Egypt, Syria, and Asia Minor, seeking closeness to God. The leading anchorites later became known as the Desert Fathers. It is understood as a synonym to anchorite, ascetic, and monk.

hesychia – This Greek word means "stillness" or "inward silence, concentration combined with inward tranquility." Hesychasm is the Orthodox Church's mystical tradition of prayer. He who seeks the prayer of stillness is called a hesychast.

Homer (c. 750 BC) – This blind poet was credited with the composition of *The Iliad* and *The Odyssey.*

icon – A holy image, usually painted on wood, adorning Orthodox churches.

komvoskoini – An Orthodox rosary or prayer rope used in counting prayers, comparable to Roman Catholic rosary beads, Muslin *tasbih,* or Buddhist and Hindu *malas.* It is a woolen string of knots, usually black and consisting of 100 knots. A cross is usually woven into the end, with a tassel for wiping away tears.

kyrie eleison - "Lord, have mercy upon us," an ancient Greek litany, probably of Hebrew origin, found in nearly all rituals for administration of Holy Communion. In the Roman Catholic Mass it follows the Introit. In liturgical churches it is generally chanted in nine-fold recitation during celebration of the Eucharist.

Lavra – An ancient term for a monastery that became a title given to the first monastery in Athos.

monk – Its origin is from the Greek word *monahos,* meaning "solitary or single one." It is understood as a synonym to *hermit, ascetic,* and *anchorite.*

mystery cults – Cults with initiation rites and conformed to general pagan expectations of piety.

nave – The main body of a church where the congregation stands.

Origen (185-254 AD) – In 225 AD he composed *On First Principles.* This is the emergence of Christian theology.

Orthodox – The term means "correct" and is used to designate the Greek-speaking church of the Byzantine Empire, acknowledging the spiritual authority of the patriarch of Constantinople.

patriarch – The Orthodox faith, differently from Roman Catholicism, is a family of self-governing churches, organized by patriarchates, which are held together by unity in the faith and communion in the sacraments. Patriarch is the title given to the higher authority of each of the self-governing churches.

Philokalia – (Greek: "Love of Beauty") The great classic of Orthodox teaching on prayer. It is an anthology of teachings by various writers from the 4th to the 15th centuries, compiled by Saint Nicodemos and Macarius Notaras, and first published in 1782.

Photius – Patriarch of Constantinople (858-867; 876-886). He revived serious study of Plato.

Plato (428-347 BC) – Plato can be considered the founder of rational philosophy. His two supreme achievements were the establishment of the Academy and the immortalizing of Socrates in writing. Both have profoundly influenced the Western world.

proskynesis - The Greek word for pilgrimage, means "prostration or veneration." It stresses what you do when you arrive rather than on how you got there.

Pythagoras (560-525 BC) – Famous for his theorem, he founded a philosophical school in Croton in southern Italy. He sought to determine the universe's harmony in the study of music and mathematics.

relics – The saints' bodily remains. The veneration of relics is a practice dating to the early church and that can be observed both in the Orthodox and Roman Catholic Churches. It is believed that a power resides in the bodily remains of the saints that can benefit the faithful who come closer.

symantron – A long wooden plank hit by a mallet and used, instead of a bell, to summon monks and pilgrims to prayer.

talanto –An iron bar used, instead of a bell, to summon monks and pilgrims to prayer.

Xerxes (486-465 BC) – King of Persia. He invaded Greece in 480 BC and suffered a defeat that compromised the integrity of the empire.

ILLUSTRATIONS